Quantitative Ammunition Selection

Charles Schwartz

Quantitative Ammunition Selection

iUniverse books may be ordered through booksellers or by contacting:

iUniverse
1663 Liberty Drive
Bloomington, IN 47403
www.iuniverse.com
844-349-9409

Because of the dynamic nature of the Internet, any web addresses or links contained in this book may have changed since publication and may no longer be valid. The views expressed in this work are solely those of the author and do not necessarily reflect the views of the publisher, and the publisher hereby disclaims any responsibility for them.

Any people depicted in stock imagery provided by Thinkstock are models, and such images are being used for illustrative purposes only.
Certain stock imagery © Thinkstock.

ISBN: 978-1-4759-2904-1 (sc)
ISBN: 978-1-4759-2906-5 (hc)
ISBN: 978-1-4759-2905-8 (e)

Library of Congress Control Number: 2012909891

Print information available on the last page.

iUniverse rev. date: 09/06/2021

For my father, Bruce, my mother, Charline,
my son, Walter, and my daughter, Genevieve

"It can scarcely be denied that the supreme goal of all theory is to make the irreducible basic elements as simple and as few as possible without having to surrender the adequate representation of a single datum of experience."

—*Albert Einstein*

Contents

1

Introduction

    While many U.S. law enforcement agencies have policies that authorize their sworn law enforcement personnel to select and carry approved non-issue firearms and ammunition while off-duty or during assignments that require the use of non-issue firearms, very few provide technical guidance to their personnel during the process of ammunition selection. After earning a bachelor's degree in psychology from Ohio State University, I entered the profession of law enforcement and found myself shortly thereafter to be in need of technical guidance in the selection of off-duty ammunition from a relatively diverse list of approved ammunition. Lacking that guidance during the selection process, I made a selection from the agency's list of pre-approved non-issue ammunition and carried it faithfully in my off-duty pistol.

    More than two decades after that defining moment in my law enforcement career, an extensive background in statistical analysis developed over the course of my career and a life-long fascination with physics that culminated with a minor in that discipline has allowed me to devise the quantitative soft tissue penetration modeling presented in the following pages. Having personally experienced the demand for such a predictive instrument, I believe that there is a genuine need for valid, translational, mathematical modeling that will allow armed professionals, under-funded agencies, and lawfully armed citizens to test, evaluate, and select self-defense ammunition that is the most appropriate to their respective tactical environments.

Once a handgun and caliber has been selected, the selection of appropriate self-defense ammunition becomes the next important consideration for the armed professional. Because it is a decision upon which the armed professional's life may depend, the selection of self-defense ammunition is a deeply personal choice. This choice is often fraught with a vast array of confusing variables and considerations that require thoughtful deliberation and research in order to ensure the selection of an appropriate projectile design. For these reasons, the need for an easily understandable process for self-defense ammunition evaluation and selection becomes apparent.

Model Design Constraints

During the 20th century, several mathematical models were offered with the intent of qualifying and quantifying the effects of the ballistic wounding mechanism: tissue permanently damaged through direct contact with the projectile. Some of these models were comprised of arbitrary collections of variables and contrived mathematical arrangements capable of producing equally arbitrary, dimensionless yields. Dimensionless yields are of little practical utility to the armed professional because they offer no meaningful context for objective comparison and lack the technical intricacy necessary to describe correctly the ballistic wounding mechanism and its effects. While some of the older, technically nuanced models offer valuable insight into the nature of the ballistic wounding mechanism, they often exceed the grasp of those lacking the technical proficiency necessary to comprehend and apply such esoteric models.

A valid quantitative model should be the unified product of the correct analysis and interpretation of empirical data and the fundamental laws of physics. It should also exhibit a high degree of correlation when compared to a large body of manufacturer- and laboratory-generated test data.

Ultimately, a valid mathematical predictive instrument must originate from conceptually sound equations and yield its results in real units of measurement, not arbitrary or dimensionless numbers. In this case, any proposed mathematical model should accept its input variables and yields its results in SI (*Système International d'Unitès*) units of measurement, a unitary system that is easily convertible to English units of measurement when necessary. The model should also describe in plain language a method of testing and evaluating self-defense ammunition with a minimal logistic and technical burden. In addition to adhering to these requirements, the model must remain easily understandable, utilize definite, uncomplicated input variables, and offer an operational procedure that is easy to learn and quick to execute. The quantitative models presented in this book meet all of these requirements.

With this objective in mind, the proposed mathematical modeling found in this book is intended to provide armed professionals and under-funded law enforcement agencies with a valid, understandable predictive mathematical instrument that will generate water test data that is directly comparable to test data obtained through the technically burdensome procedure of conducting ballistic tests in shear-validated 10-percent ordnance gelatin. Toward that end, the following chapters provide a concise explanation of the relevant principles of mechanics, fluid dynamics, and thermodynamics that pertain to such modeling and its derivation as well as numerous clearly illustrated examples that demonstrate every aspect of its implementation.

2

Fundamental Principles

In this chapter, the principles of mechanics, fluid dynamics, and thermodynamics will be discussed as they pertain to the development and application of the terminal ballistic performance model. This is intended to provide the armed professional with an informed perspective of the phenomena involved in projectile motion through a homogenous fluid or hydrocolloidal medium.

Through comparative analysis, the dynamic equivalence (in terms of respective density and internal speed of sound) of water and shear-validated 10-percent ordnance gelatin as ballistic test mediums will be established.

Mechanics

The first principle of mechanics relevant to the mathematical model is Newton's first law of motion which states that, once in motion, an object of mass, m, will remain at the same velocity, v, until it is acted upon by an exterior force, F.

Corollary to this, an object at rest remains at rest until it is acted upon by an exterior force. Both conditions illustrate the concept that is qualitatively known as the property of inertia.

This law of mechanics is illustrated through the simple example of a ball thrown through the air from one person to another. After the ball is thrown, the effects of gravity and air resistance dictate its path, or trajectory. Gravity acts upon the ball causing it to accelerate (or fall) towards the Earth and the force of frictional resistance from the air (which is a fluid) acts

4

upon the surface of the ball causing it to decelerate immediately after it is thrown. If these exterior forces were not present, the ball would continue to move in a straight line at the same velocity forever or until another exterior force acts upon it.

The second principle of mechanics that pertains to the mathematical model is Newton's second law of motion expressed by the equation

$$F = ma,$$

which states that an exterior force, F, acting upon an object having a mass, m, will induce in that object an acceleration, a, inversely proportional to the object's mass, m, until the exterior force ceases to act upon the object.

Conversely, if a directly opposing exterior force, $-F$, acts upon the object of mass, m, moving at an initially acquired velocity, v_o, a deceleration, $-a$, inversely proportional to the mass, m, of the object results, subsequently reducing the object's initially acquired velocity, v_o. Given a sufficient period of time, Δt, for the opposing force, $-F$, to act upon the mass, a reversal of the object's velocity, $-v$, will eventually occur.

Using the prior example of the ball thrown from one person to another provides an excellent illustration of both aspects of this physical law. The force exerted upon the ball as it is thrown from one person to another accelerates the ball to a velocity that is proportional to the force exerted upon it by the hand from which it is thrown.

Conversely, as the person to whom the ball was thrown catches the ball, the hand used to catch the ball must exert a force upon it that opposes the ball's forward motion, causing it to decelerate and come to a stop. If the ball is to be thrown back to the person who first threw it, a successful return requires that an equal and opposite force must be exerted upon it, causing an acceleration that is the opposite of the first and imparting an equally opposing velocity (and trajectory) to the ball.

The third principle of mechanics that applies to the mathematical model is Newton's third law of motion which states, "To every action there is an equal and opposite reaction." This relationship is expressed by the equation

$$mv = mv$$

and is known as the law of conservation of momentum.

Since an exterior force, F, applied to a mass, m, produces an acceleration, a, over a period of time, Δt, (the time rate of change of velocity),

$$F = ma = m(\Delta v/\Delta t),$$

it may be deduced that force also causes a change in the momentum of an object, Δp, over a period of time, Δt. This vector quantity, the time rate of change of momentum, is expressed as

$$F = \Delta p/\Delta t.$$

During the acceleration or deceleration (the time rate of change of velocity) induced by the action of an exterior force upon an object, the distance traveled by the object during its acceleration or deceleration may be expressed by the equation

$$S = V^2/2a,$$

which, with proper modification in a subsequent chapter, will permit the prediction of the maximum terminal penetration depth of a projectile.

Once an object of mass, m, acquires a velocity, v, it possesses both momentum, p,

$$p = mv,$$

and kinetic energy, E_K, expressed as the indefinite integral of momentum, p,

$$E_K = \int p \, \delta v = \int mv \, \delta v = \tfrac{1}{2}mv^2.$$

While a projectile in motion possesses both momentum and kinetic energy, the penetration of a transient projectile through a homogenous fluid or hydrocolloidal medium constitutes an inelastic collision that is correctly treated as a momentum transaction. Therefore, a momentum-based analysis of projectile motion is the most equitable approach in constructing a mathematical terminal ballistic model.

Although it may be possible to devise a mathematical terminal ballistic model based upon the expenditure of a projectile's kinetic energy as it traverses a medium, there is nothing to be gained from the pursuit of such an unnecessarily complex approach.

Fluid Dynamics

The first principle of fluid dynamics relevant to the terminal ballistic model is the effect of viscous and inertial drag force components upon a projectile as it passes through a homogenous fluid or hydrocolloidal test medium. Viscous (or frictional) drag is the predominant form of drag encountered by projectiles moving through fluids and gases at low velocities. It is produced by the direct contact of the fluid or gas acting upon the surfaces of a projectile. Inertial drag is the predominant form of drag encountered by projectiles traversing fluids at relatively high velocities. It is produced by the fluid's inertia in opposition to the projectile's motion.

Flow field regimes are quantified and qualified by a Reynolds number, R_e, which is a dimensionless parameter that is expressed as the ratio of inertial drag forces to viscous (or frictional) drag forces encountered by a projectile as it traverses a fluid medium. The relationship is described by the equation

$$R_e = \rho V D / \mu,$$

where ρ is the density of the medium in grams per cubic centimeter, V is the velocity of the flow field in centimeters per second relative to the transient projectile, D is the diameter of the projectile in centimeters, and μ is the dynamic viscosity of the medium expressed in grams per centimeter·second, or poise, an SI unit of measurement.

The magnitude of a Reynolds number qualifies the flow field surrounding a transient projectile as being either laminar or turbulent and determines whether viscous or inviscid equations are applicable to the analysis of the flow field relative to the passage of a transient projectile. Laminar flow fields are characterized as having uniformly smooth, consistent motion with no lateral currents or flow disruptions. Turbulent flow fields are characterized as having random flow irregularities and chaotic flow vortices that exceed the intrinsic viscous dampening properties of the medium being traversed.

At impact and transient projectile velocities of 300 feet per second to 1,700 feet per second, the Reynolds number of flow fields relative to the passage of typical, non-expanding and expanding service-caliber projectiles through water ranges from 500,000 to more than 16,000,000. Reynolds numbers of this magnitude indicate that turbulent flow field regimes predominate over this range of projectile velocities. Accordingly, inviscid equations are appropriate for modeling the behavior of high- and low-velocity service-caliber projectiles traversing homogenous fluids, such as water, and thixotropic (the material property of liquefying when subjected to pressure) hydrocolloidal mediums, such as shear-validated 10-percent ordnance gelatin.

The second principle of fluid dynamics that pertains to the mathematical model is the production of dynamic pressure, P_D, arising from the impingement of a projectile in motion upon a hydrocolloidal soft tissue simulant (shear-validated 10-percent ordnance gelatin) as compared to the dynamic pressure produced by a projectile traversing a homogenous fluid medium (water). The dynamic pressure, expressed as force per unit of area, produced by a projectile's motion through a medium is responsible for driving projectile expansion and ultimately dictates the terminal penetration depth of the projectile. In order to establish the dynamic equivalence of the two mediums, it is possible to compare the respective dynamic pressures produced in both mediums using the equation

$$P_D = \tfrac{1}{2}\rho V^2.$$

Since the respective densities of water (999.972 kg/m^3) and shear-validated 10-percent ordnance gelatin (1,040 ± 20.00 kg/m^3) have already been established, it may be demonstrated with little difficulty that the dynamic pressures produced by identical projectiles at identical velocities are 4.00 ± 2.00 percent greater in shear-validated 10-percent ordnance gelatin than in water. While the difference between the pressures produced within the two mediums is not insignificant, it is also not enough to preclude the use of water as a valid test medium when the totality of its properties are weighed against those of shear-validated 10-percent ordnance gelatin.

Thermodynamics

The first thermodynamic principle relevant to the mathematical model is the internal speed of sound, V_s, within each respective test medium. This physical property is inversely proportional to the density, ρ, of the medium and directly proportional to the compressibility of the medium, expressed by the adiabatic (relating to an "isolated" system into which no additional energy is introduced from an outside source) bulk modulus, K, which has its units in pressure (pascals or newtons per meter^2).

It is possible to compare the speed of sound in water and shear-validated 10-percent ordnance gelatin through the constitutive relationship that is described by the Newton-Laplace formula,

$$V_s = \sqrt{(K \div \rho)}.$$

By applying the values for the density of water, 999.972 kg/m^3 at 39.2°F/4°C, and the adiabatic bulk modulus (K) of water, 2.24 x 10^9 Pa, to the prior equation, the speed of sound through water may be calculated as:

$$V_s = \sqrt{(2.24 \times 10^9 \text{ Pa} \div 999.972 \text{ kg/m}^3)}$$

$$V_s = 1{,}496.68 \text{ mps or } 4{,}910.38 \text{ fps.}$$

The density of properly prepared shear-validated 10-percent ordnance gelatin at 39.2°F/4°C is 1,040 ± 20.00 kg/m^3. Since water is the predominant component (90 percent) of shear-validated 10-percent ordnance gelatin, it is reasonable to expect that the adiabatic bulk modulus (K) of shear-validated 10-percent ordnance gelatin, 2.32 x 10^9 Pa, is very close to that of water. The calculation for the speed of sound within shear-validated 10-percent ordnance gelatin is then:

$$V_s = \sqrt{(2.32 \times 10^9 \text{ Pa} \div 1{,}040 \pm 20.00 \text{ kg/m}^3)}$$

V_s = 1,493.78 mps ± 14.36 mps or 4,900.85 ± 47.11 fps.

Through this comparative analysis, it becomes apparent that both water and shear-validated 10-percent ordnance gelatin have a virtually identical internal speed of sound, the difference being approximately fifty feet per second, or about one percent.

Although all fluids exhibit varying degrees of compressibility, compressibility effects such as transonic drag rise, which are dependent upon the speed of sound within a medium, may be considered to be negligible when transient projectile velocities do not exceed one third of the speed of sound within the medium (1,635 feet per second in water and shear-validated 10-percent ordnance gelatin). For this reason, the terminal ballistic performance of handgun projectiles in water, shear-validated 10-percent ordnance gelatin, and soft tissue is correctly modeled as occurring within an incompressible subsonic flow regime.

The second thermodynamic principle that pertains to the mathematical model is that of the conversion of kinetic energy to thermal energy within an adiabatic system. As stated earlier, the kinetic energy possessed by an object in motion is expressed by the equation

$$E_K = \frac{1}{2}mv^2$$

which has its units in joules (newton·meter), an SI unit of measurement.

When a projectile having a known kinetic energy strikes and comes to rest within a medium having a constant volume (isochoric) and mass, it is possible to determine the increase in temperature within the system that is produced by the conversion of the projectile's (mechanical) kinetic energy into thermal energy.

By way of extreme example, consider a hypothetical adiabatic system consisting of a .50-caliber (0.500 inch in diameter) rifle projectile having a mass of 700 grains (one tenth of a pound) and a velocity of 2,850 feet per second striking and coming to rest inside of a block of shear-validated 10-percent ordnance gelatin after traversing its entire length. The block, measuring one and a half inches on a side and twelve inches in length, would weigh approximately one pound and would simulate the proximate cross-section of soft tissue that would be impinged upon by such a projectile traversing a human torso twelve inches in depth.

Even though it is certain that such a narrow block of gelatin would be torn apart by the large mechanical forces of such an impact, it must be assumed for the purpose of this example that the narrow block of gelatin would remain intact as the projectile expends one hundred percent of its kinetic energy within the block of gelatin. Because it takes 1,055.05 joules (one British thermal unit or BTU) of the projectile's total kinetic energy (17,114.15

joules) to raise the temperature of one pound of shear-validated 10-percent ordnance gelatin by one degree Fahrenheit, the result of such a hypothetical experiment would be that the temperature of the gelatin block would increase by approximately 16.2° Fahrenheit.

The latent heat of vaporization of water (the energy required to convert one kilogram of water into steam from body temperature, 98.6° Fahrenheit, is 2,521 kJ) is more than 600 times greater than the specific heat of water (the amount of energy required to raise the temperature of one kilogram of water by one degree Centigrade is 4.179 kJ). For this reason, it may be deduced with a high degree of confidence that any thermal effect attributable to the conversion of the transient projectile's kinetic energy into thermal energy during its passage through soft tissue would be inconsequential when compared to the mechanical effects produced by the passage of the transient projectile. In the simplest terms, the kinetic energy possessed by a handgun or rifle projectile is insufficient to contribute significantly to the ballistic wounding mechanism through the thermal vaporization of soft tissue.

Dynamic Equivalence of the Mediums

In "Applied Wound Ballistics: What's New and What's True", the authors describe the use of water as an acceptable tissue simulant, citing the U.S. Federal Bureau of Investigation Firearms Training Unit's use of water as a screening mechanism in the evaluation of ammunition:

Water can be used as a tissue simulant and causes just slightly more bullet deformation than gelatin or soap; the Firearms Training Unit of the U.S. Federal Bureau of Investigation uses it as a screening mechanism to decide which bullets expand well enough to merit further scrutiny.

Because water slightly overdrives the deformation of expanding projectile designs, it serves as an excellent discriminator for eliminating those designs that may offer marginal performance in mediums like shear-validated 10-percent ordnance gelatin and human soft tissue that tend to produce slightly lower rates of projectile deformation.

Upon consideration of the comparative analysis presented herein, it should be evident that water possesses dynamic qualities (a similar density and a virtually identical internal speed of sound) that are nearly identical to those of shear-validated 10-percent ordnance gelatin making water suitable for use as a terminal ballistic test medium.

3

The Model and Its Derivation

When a projectile strikes and traverses shear-validated 10-percent ordnance gelatin, soft tissue, or water, it encounters a decelerative force in the form of drag, F_D.

The magnitude of the drag force, F_D, encountered by the projectile is directly proportional to the density, ρ, of the medium being traversed, the projectile's coefficient of drag, C_D, the cross-sectional area, A_{cs}, of the presented projectile face, and to the square of the instantaneous velocity, V^2, of the projectile at any point of its travel through the medium. Drag acts continuously upon the impinging projectile while the projectile is in motion through the target medium causing it to decelerate until its velocity falls below the elastic limit, V_L, of the target medium. The elastic limit of a medium is defined as the lowest velocity at which a projectile of a given density, ρ_p (in kg/m³), will continue to move forward through a medium. It is expressed in terms of projectile velocity (in meters per second) in the equation

$$V_L = \sqrt{[2(\sigma_t \div \rho_p)]}.$$

When the dynamic pressure, P_D (in N/m²), produced by the projectile's movement through the medium falls below the yield strength, σ_t (in N/m²), of the target medium, the projectile comes to rest.

As a projectile penetrates soft tissue or a hydrocolloidal medium its forward "wetted" surface displaces material radially upon direct contact in and along its path. The majority of the material making direct contact with the leading surface of the transient projectile will be permanently damaged. This creates a permanent wound cavity that has a volume and mass that is directly proportional to the diameter and momentum of the transient projectile. The passage of a projectile through a homogenous fluid or hydrocolloidal medium under these conditions constitutes a momentum transaction. Therefore, the model's central mathematical argument rests upon Newton's second law of motion as its foundation.

The primary elements of the ballistic wounding mechanism: terminal penetration depth, S, and the mass contained within the volume of the permanent wound cavity, M_{PC}, may be predicted by applying the input variables of average recovered projectile diameter, D, recovered projectile mass, M, and the impact velocity of the projectile, V_i, to the quantitative modeling described herein.

While temporary cavitation may contribute to the potential wounding capacity (permanently damaged tissue) of a transient projectile over the range of typical service-caliber velocities (700 to 1,500 feet per second), it is usually of insufficient magnitude to exceed the yield strength of many, if not most, of the soft tissues that it impinges upon. For this reason, temporary cavitation cannot be relied upon to contribute to the efficacy of the ballistic wounding mechanism. As a result, the highly variable and unreliable nature of temporary cavitation warrants its exclusion from consideration in the mathematical model.

Model Derivation

The equation of motion of the terminal ballistic performance model is predicated upon Newton's second law of motion expressed by the equation

$$F = m(\Delta v/\Delta t) = ma,$$

where a equals the acceleration produced by a force, F, acting upon a projectile's mass, m.

Rearranging the equation $F = ma$, to solve for a, yields

$$a = F/m.$$

The drag force, F_D, acting upon a projectile as it traverses a fluid or hydrocolloidal medium is expressed by the equation

$$F_D = \tfrac{1}{2}\rho V^2 C_D A_{cs},$$

where ρ is the density of the fluid or hydrocolloidal medium, V is the instantaneous velocity of the projectile at any point along its path of travel through the medium, C_D is the projectile's drag coefficient, and A_{cs} is the cross-sectional area (in centimeters^2) presented by the projectile.

The equation for drag force (F_D) may then be used to modify $a = F/m$ by direct substitution so that

$$a = \tfrac{1}{2}\rho V^2 C_D A_{cs}/m.$$

The total distance traversed by a projectile during its deceleration within a medium may be expressed as

$$S = V^2/2a.$$

Substituting the expression, $\tfrac{1}{2}\rho V^2 C_D A_{cs}/m$, equivalent to a in the prior equation, yields

$$S = V^2/2(\tfrac{1}{2}\rho V^2 C_D A_{cs}/m),$$

which, after all extraneous terms have been reduced, becomes the model's primary mathematical argument,

$$S = m \div A_{cs}\rho C_D.$$

The governing expression for the model's primary mathematical argument,

$$LN\ [(V \div \epsilon)^2 + 1],$$

relies upon a uniaxial strain proportionality, ϵ, which scales to the cube root of the projectile's diameter, D, the ultimate tensile strength of soft tissue, σ_t, and the density of soft tissue, ρ_t,

$$\epsilon = \sqrt[3]{D} \times \sqrt{(\sigma_t \div \rho_t)}$$

The governing expression, multiplied by the primary mathematical argument, yields the solution for the terminal penetration depth, S, of a projectile in shear-validated 10-percent ordnance gelatin or soft tissue,

$$S = LN\ [(V \div \epsilon)^2 + 1] \times [m \div (A_{cs}\rho C_D)].$$

When $V \div \epsilon$ is less than or equal to one, viscous (frictional) drag force components dominate the flow regime. When $V \div \epsilon$ is greater than one, inertial drag force components begin to dominate the flow regime. As $V \div \epsilon$ approaches ∞, the effect of viscous drag force components vanishes rendering the flow field relative to the transient projectile inviscid.

The Quantitative Model

The quantitative model is presented in this section along with a table of parameter values (C_D and Φ) and a definition of all variables for the sake of clarity.

Terminal Penetration

$$S = LN\ [(V_i \div \epsilon)^2 + 1] \times [M \div (\pi \times (\tfrac{1}{2}D_{cm})^2 \times \rho \times C_D)]$$

where $\epsilon = \sqrt[3]{D_{mm}} \times \sqrt{(\sigma_t \div \rho_t)}$

Residual Velocity

$$V_{rx} = \epsilon \times \sqrt{(e^x - 1)}$$

where $x = (S - T_F) \div [M \div (\pi \times (\tfrac{1}{2}D_{cm})^2 \times \rho \times C_D)]$

Permanent Wound Mass

$$M_{PC} = \pi \times (\tfrac{1}{2}D_{cm})^2 \times S \times \rho \times \Phi$$

Model Parameters

Projectile Configuration	C_D	Φ
Wadcutter	0.833333	1.000000
Jacketed Hollow Point	0.441511	0.819152
Full Metal Jacket Round Nose	0.573576	0.688292
Cruciform Flat Nose	0.597175	0.716610
Truncated Cone	0.551937	0.662324
Semi-Wadcutter	0.551937	0.662324
60° Conical Point	0.500000	0.600000
Round Ball	0.414214	0.497056

Model Variables

C_D = coefficient of drag

D_{mm} = average (recovered) projectile diameter (millimeters)

D_{cm} = average (recovered) projectile diameter (centimeters)

$e \approx 2.718281828459045$

LN = natural logarithm function

M = (recovered) projectile mass (grams)

M_{PC} = mass within permanent wound cavity (grams)

S = projectile terminal penetration depth (centimeters)

T_F = finite target thickness (centimeters)

T_{Fs} = skin thickness (0.100 – 0.400 centimeters)
  average skin thickness: $\approx$ 0.310 centimeters

V_i = projectile impact velocity (meters per second)

V_{rx} = projectile residual velocity (meters per second)

ϵ = uniaxial strain proportionality

Φ = projectile configuration factor

$\pi \approx 3.141592653589793$

ρ_t = density of 10% ordnance gelatin and soft tissue
  (1.040 ± 0.020 grams/cm^3 or $1{,}040 \pm 20$ kg/m^3)

ρ_{at} = density of adipose tissue
  (0.950 ± 0.025 grams/cm^3 or 950 ± 25 kg/m^3)

ρ_s = density of skin
  (1.060 ± 0.020 grams/cm^3 or $1{,}060 \pm 20$ kg/m^3)

σ_t = ultimate tensile strength of soft tissue
  ($1{,}000{,}000 \pm 100{,}000$ newtons per meter^2)

σ_{at} = ultimate tensile strength of adipose tissue
  ($321{,}000 \pm 118{,}300$ newtons per meter^2)

σ_s = ultimate tensile strength of skin
  ($7{,}580{,}000$ newtons per meter^2)

Operational Constraints

The quantitative model operates under three conditions:

- All significant plastic deformation of the projectile occurs within periods of 10^{-4} seconds.

- The projectile behaves as a rigid body after expansion (no further ductile or ablative erosion occurs) and exhibits no significant yaw during any portion of the penetration event.

- The terminal behavior of the projectile is governed by a material strength variable and by inertial and viscous (or frictional) drag losses that occur during the projectile's penetration through the medium.

When evaluated against more than 800 points of independent test data under these constraints, the quantitative model predicts the terminal penetration depth of projectiles in shear-validated 10-percent ordnance gelatin with a margin of error of one centimeter within a confidence interval of 95 percent and exhibits a correlation of $r = +0.94$.

In the next chapter, several detailed examples of the model's operation will be presented that will allow the armed professional to closely examine the actual computational process and to obtain a clear understanding of all aspects of the model's operation.

4

Model Implementation and Examples

In this chapter, several examples of the model's operation will be presented in order to permit the observation of every computational operation involved in the implementation of the mathematical model. When necessary, these examples may be used to diagnose and resolve difficulties that arise during the implementation of the quantitative model.

Minimum Required Equipment

At the absolute minimum, the armed professional should have a scientific calculator at his disposal (available at most office supply stores and priced from $15.00 to $150.00 depending upon the number of options offered) because the model's equations employ natural logarithmic, inverse natural logarithmic and variable exponential functions. These mathematical operators are usually designated on calculator keys as "LN", "e^x", and "y^x", respectively. Although it is not absolutely necessary, the calculator should also have a constant function key for the value of *pi* (п) and at least two storage memories so that prior computed values may be retained for use in later calculations.

Implementation

The model's most frequent application will be that of the straightforward process of entering the input variables of impact velocity, recovered mass, and recovered diameter to predict the terminal penetration of a test projectile and the corresponding mass of damaged soft tissue contained within the permanent wound cavity. Because firing a non-expanding projectile (such as a full metal jacket round nose bullet) into water is unnecessary (it may be reasonably assumed that a non-expanding design will not expand under such conditions), the armed professional may simply apply all input variables directly to the model and obtain a predictive result without undertaking the rigors of testing.

Occasionally, the need to predict the residual velocity of a specific projectile after it exits a target material of finite thickness may arise, but such calculations serve as an educational exercise in most cases.

Where an actual test projectile is evaluated using the model, two measurements of the recovered projectile will be required. The first is the measurement of the recovered mass of the projectile (in grams). The second is the measurement of the average expansion diameter (the average of the largest and smallest measured cross-sectional diameters) of the recovered projectile in centimeters (for use in the primary mathematical argument) and millimeters (for use in the model's governing expression).

Examples

In order to permit the greatest procedural transparency in the following examples, all computations are displayed to an unusually high degree of numerical precision.

<u>Example #1</u>

To what depth would a non-deforming, 9-millimeter (diameter = 9.017 millimeters), full metal jacket round nose (FMJRN) bullet, weighing 124 grains and having an impact velocity of 1,100 feet per second, penetrate in soft tissue that has a density of $1,040 \pm 20$ kg/m³?

First, determine the value of the uniaxial strain proportionality, ϵ:

$$\epsilon = {}^3\sqrt{D_{mm}} \times \sqrt{(\sigma_t \div \rho_t)}$$

$$\epsilon = {}^3\sqrt{9.017} \times \sqrt{(1,000,000 \div 1,040)}$$

$$\epsilon = {}^3\sqrt{9.017} \times \sqrt{(961.538462)}$$

$$\epsilon = 2.081392682 \times 31.008684$$

$$\epsilon = 64.5412.$$

Using the calculated value for ϵ, predict the maximum penetration depth (S, in centimeters) of the non-deforming, 9-millimeter bullet in soft tissue that has a density of 1.040 grams per cubic centimeter. It will be necessary to convert the velocity of the bullet, 1,100 feet per second, to meters per second (335.28 meters per second), the mass of the bullet, 124 grains, to grams (8.0351 grams), and the diameter of the bullet, 0.355 inch, to centimeters (0.9017 centimeter):

$$S = LN\ [(V_i \div \epsilon)^2 + 1] \times [M \div (\pi \times (\tfrac{1}{2}D_{cm})^2 \times \rho \times C_D)]$$

$$S = LN\ [(335.28 \div 64.5412)^2 + 1] \times [8.0351 \div (3.1415927 \times (\tfrac{1}{2} \times 0.9017)^2 \times 1.040 \times 0.573576)]$$

$$S = LN\ [(5.1948)^2 + 1] \times [8.0351 \div (0.3809)]$$

$$S = LN\ [27.9859] \times [21.095]$$

$$S = 3.3317 \times 21.095$$

$$S = 70.2822 \text{ centimeters or } 27.6702 \text{ inches.}$$

At what velocity would the non-deforming, 9-millimeter (0.9017 centimeter), 124-grain, full metal jacket round nose bullet exit the opposite side of an abdomen that has a finite thickness (T_F) of 13.00 inches (33.020 centimeters)?

First, determine the value of "x":

$$x = (S - T_F) \div [M \div (\pi \times (\tfrac{1}{2}D_{cm})^2 \times \rho \times C_D)]$$

$$x = (70.2822 - 33.020) \div [8.0351 \div (3.1415927 \times (\tfrac{1}{2} \times 0.9017)^2 \times 1.040 \times 0.573576)]$$

$$x = (36.2622) \div [8.0351 \div (0.3809)]$$

$$x = (36.2622) \div [21.095]$$

$$x = 1.7664.$$

Next, predict the residual (exit) velocity of the bullet by substituting the value 1.7664 for "x" in the following equation:

$$V_{rx} = \epsilon \times \sqrt{(e^x - 1)}$$

$$V_{rx} = 64.5412 \times \sqrt{(2.7182818285^{\,1.7664} - 1)}$$

$$V_{rx} = 64.5412 \times \sqrt{(5.8498 - 1)}$$

$$V_{rx} = 64.5412 \times \sqrt{(4.8498)}$$

$$V_{rx} = 64.5412 \times 2.2022$$

$$V_{rx} = 142.1326 \text{ meters per second or}$$
$$466.3143 \text{ feet per second.}$$

Using the calculated value for ϵ, predict the maximum penetration depth of the non-deforming, 9-millimeter (diameter = 0.9017 centimeter), full metal jacket round nose bullet, weighing 124 grains (8.0351 grams) and having an impact velocity of 300 feet per second (91.44 meters per second), in soft tissue that has a density of 1.040 grams per cubic centimeter:

$$S = LN\ [(V_i \div \epsilon)^2 + 1] \times [M \div (\pi \times (\tfrac{1}{2}D_{cm})^2 \times \rho \times C_D)]$$

$$S = LN\ [(91.44 \div 64.5412)^2 + 1] \times [8.0351 \div$$
$$(3.1415927 \times (\tfrac{1}{2} \times 0.9017)^2 \times 1.040 \times 0.573576)]$$

$$S = LN\ [(1.4168)^2 + 1] \times [8.0351 \div (0.3809)]$$

$$S = LN\ [3.0073] \times [21.095]$$

$$S = 1.10104 \times 21.095$$

$$S = 23.2264 \text{ centimeters or } 9.1443 \text{ inches.}$$

Example #2

A .45 ACP (Automatic Colt Pistol) jacketed hollow point bullet, weighing 230 grains (14.9038 grams), strikes and passes through a heavy clothing barrier before entering a water test medium at a velocity of 865 feet per second (263.652 meters per second). After expanding to an average diameter of 0.735 inch (18.669 millimeters or 1.8669 centimeters), it comes to rest and retains 229.2 grains (14.8519 grams) of its initial 230-grain mass. To what depth would the bullet penetrate in soft tissue that has a density of 1,040 ± 20 kg/m^3?

First, determine the value of the uniaxial strain proportionality, ϵ:

$$\epsilon = {}^3\sqrt{D_{mm}} \times \sqrt{(\sigma_t \div \rho_t)}$$

$$\epsilon = {}^3\sqrt{18.669} \times \sqrt{(1,000,000 \div 1,040)}$$

$$\epsilon = {}^3\sqrt{18.669} \times \sqrt{(961.538462)}$$

$$\epsilon = 2.652815330 \times 31.008684$$

$$\epsilon = 82.2603.$$

Using the calculated value for ϵ, predict the maximum penetration depth of the expanded, 229.2-grain (14.8519 grams), jacketed hollow point bullet in soft tissue that has a density of 1.040 grams per cubic centimeter:

$$S = LN\ [(V_i \div \epsilon)^2 + 1] \times [M \div (\pi \times (\tfrac{1}{2}D_{cm})^2 \times \rho \times C_D)]$$

$$S = LN\ [(263.652 \div 82.2603)^2 + 1] \times [14.8519 \div (3.1415927 \times (\tfrac{1}{2} \times 1.8669)^2 \times 1.040 \times 0.441511)]$$

$$S = LN\ [(3.2051)^2 + 1] \times [14.8519 \div (1.2569)]$$

$$S = LN\ [11.2727] \times [11.8163]$$

$$S = 2.4224 \times 11.8163$$

S = 28.6238 centimeters or 11.2692 inches.

At what velocity would the expanded, .45 ACP, jacketed hollow point bullet (with a recovered mass of 229.2 grains) exit the opposite side of an abdomen having a thickness (T_F) of 9.00 inches (22.860 centimeters)?

First, determine the value of "x":

$$x = (S - T_F) \div [M \div (\pi \times (\tfrac{1}{2}D_{cm})^2 \times \rho \times C_D)]$$

$$x = (28.6238 - 22.860) \div [14.8519 \div (3.1415927 \times (\tfrac{1}{2} \times 1.8669)^2 \times 1.040 \times 0.441511)]$$

$$x = (5.7638) \div [14.8519 \div (1.2569)]$$

$$x = (5.7638) \div [11.8163]$$

$$x = 0.4882.$$

Next, predict the residual (exit) velocity of the bullet by substituting the value 0.4882 for "x" in the following equation:

$$V_{rx} = \epsilon \times \sqrt{(e^x - 1)}$$

$$V_{rx} = 82.2603 \times \sqrt{(2.7182818285^{\,0.4882} - 1)}$$

$$V_{rx} = 82.2603 \times \sqrt{(1.6294 - 1)}$$

$$V_{rx} = 82.2603 \times \sqrt{(0.6294)}$$

$$V_{rx} = 82.2603 \times 0.7933$$

V_{rx} = 65.2571 meters per second or
214.0981 feet per second.

Assume that the .45 ACP jacketed hollow point bullet was fired into, and remained inside of, an abdomen (after expanding to 0.735 inch or 1.8669 centimeters) having a thickness (T_F) of 14.00 inches and a density of 1.040 grams per cubic centimeter. What would be the total mass of the permanent wound cavity (M_{PC}) produced by the expanded bullet remaining inside of the abdomen?

Determine the mass within the permanent wound cavity (M_{PC}) produced by the bullet's passage:

$$M_{PC} = \pi \times (\tfrac{1}{2}D_{cm})^2 \times S \times \rho \times \Phi$$

$$M_{PC} = 3.1415927 \times (\tfrac{1}{2} \times 1.8669)^2 \times 28.6238 \times 1.040 \times 0.819152$$

$$M_{PC} = 3.1415927 \times 0.8713 \times 28.6238 \times 1.040 \times 0.819152$$

$$M_{PC} = 66.7487 \text{ grams or } 2.3545 \text{ ounces.}$$

Example #3

A 10-millimeter jacketed hollow point bullet weighing 155 grains is fired at a velocity of 1,420 feet per second (432.816 meters per second) through a light-weight clothing barrier and recovered from a water test medium. It expands radically to a diameter of 0.814 inch (20.6756 millimeters or 2.06756 centimeters) and loses 14.26 percent of its initial mass for a recovered mass of 132.9 grains (8.6118 grams). To what depth would it penetrate in soft tissue that has a density of $1{,}040 \pm 20$ kg/m³?

First, determine the value of the uniaxial strain proportionality, ϵ:

$$\epsilon = \sqrt[3]{D_{mm}} \times \sqrt{(\sigma_t \div \rho_t)}$$

$$\epsilon = \sqrt[3]{20.6756} \times \sqrt{(1{,}000{,}000 \div 1{,}040)}$$

$$\epsilon = \sqrt[3]{20.6756} \times \sqrt{(961.538462)}$$

$$\epsilon = 2.7446 \times 31.008684$$

$$\epsilon = 85.1064.$$

Using the calculated value for ϵ, predict the maximum penetration depth of the expanded, 132.9-grain (8.6118 grams), jacketed hollow point bullet in soft tissue that has a density of 1.040 grams per cubic centimeter:

$$S = LN\left[(V_i \div \epsilon)^2 + 1\right] \times \left[M \div (\pi \times (\tfrac{1}{2}D_{cm})^2 \times \rho \times C_D)\right]$$

$$S = LN\left[(432.816 \div 85.1064)^2 + 1\right] \times \left[8.6118 \div (3.1415927 \times (\tfrac{1}{2} \times 2.06756)^2 \times 1.040 \times 0.441511)\right]$$

$$S = LN\left[(5.0865)^2 + 1\right] \times \left[8.6118 \div (1.5416)\right]$$

$$S = LN\left[26.8633\right] \times \left[5.5863\right]$$

$$S = \left[3.2908\right] \times \left[5.5863\right]$$

$$S = 18.3834 \text{ centimeters or } 7.2376 \text{ inches.}$$

Assume that the 10-millimeter jacketed hollow point bullet was fired into, and remains inside of, an abdomen (after expanding to 0.814 inch or 2.06756 centimeters) having a thickness (T_F) of 13.00 inches and a density of 1.040 grams per cubic centimeter. What would be the total mass of the permanent wound cavity (M_{PC}) produced by the expanded bullet remaining inside of the abdomen?

Determine the mass within the permanent wound cavity (M_{PC}) produced by the bullet's passage:

$$M_{PC} = \Pi \times (\tfrac{1}{2}D_{cm})^2 \times S \times \rho \times \Phi$$

$$M_{PC} = 3.1415927 \times (\tfrac{1}{2} \times 2.06756)^2 \times 18.3834 \times 1.040 \times 0.819152$$

$$M_{PC} = 3.1415927 \times 1.0687 \times 18.3834 \times 1.040 \times 0.819152$$

$$M_{PC} = 52.5811 \text{ grams or } 1.8547 \text{ ounces.}$$

The mathematical model may be used to predict the terminal ballistic performance of both existing and conceptual projectiles composed of exotic alloys and materials. Such application requires the estimation of input variables when no actual projectile is physically available for such measurement. The process for estimating these input variables is addressed in the following chapter and accompanied by detailed examples meant to illustrate clearly the model's utility in such applications.

5

Modeling Exotic Projectile Performance

The mathematical model may be used to evaluate the terminal ballistic performance of projectiles composed of exotic alloys and materials. In order to apply the model correctly, the input variables of recovered projectile mass, impact velocity, and recovered projectile diameter must be determined through direct measurement. In cases where conceptual projectile designs are to be evaluated hypothetically, the values of the input variables must be estimated using proven mathematical relationships.

Estimation of Projectile Properties

Where an actual measurement (initial and recovered mass, average recovered diameter) should be taken from an existing projectile, the determination of these variables may also be estimated where no actual projectile is available.

The process of estimating the composite density (ρ_c) of a conceptual projectile design relies upon the presumption that the composite density of a projectile is proportionally adjusted for each component material or alloy present in the construction of the projectile under consideration.

Jacketed hollow point projectiles of current manufacture consist of a lead-alloy core (typically 0.25 percent to 3 percent antimonial lead) that has been either forcibly inserted into the pre-formed jacket under high pressure or bonded to the jacket by an electro-chemical or thermal-bonding process. Projectile jackets are usually composed of a copper-based alloy, such as "gilding metal" (95 percent copper and 5 percent zinc) or "cartridge brass" (70 percent copper and 30 percent zinc), and usually comprise 12 percent to 18 percent of the projectile's total mass with the remaining balance being that of the projectile's lead-alloy core.

Given a jacketed hollow point projectile that has a full-length, "gilding metal" jacket (ρ = 8.869 grams/cm^3) that constitutes 15 percent of its mass and a 2 percent antimonial lead core (ρ = 11.241 grams/cm^3) that makes up the remaining 85 percent of the projectile's mass, the composite density of the jacketed hollow point projectile would be:

$$\rho_c = (0.85 \times 11.241 \text{ g/cm}^3) + (0.15 \times 8.869 \text{ g/cm}^3)$$

$$\rho_c = 10.885 \text{ g/cm}^3.$$

It is then possible to estimate, with reasonable accuracy, the volume of the projectile and, using the density of another alloy or material, estimate the mass of the conceptual projectile.

For example, the volume of a conceptual projectile that is to be fabricated of pure zinc and duplicates the configuration and volume of a 185-grain (11.9878 grams), .45-caliber, jacketed hollow point projectile (of conventional construction) would be:

$$11.9878 \text{ grams} \div 10.885 \text{ g/cm}^3 = 1.1013 \text{ cm}^3.$$

Multiplying the density of the material being substituted (the density of zinc is 7.140 grams/cm^3) times the estimated volume of the projectile design yields the estimated mass of the conceptual projectile:

$$1.1013 \text{ cm}^3 \times 7.140 \text{ g/cm}^3 = 7.8633$$
$$\text{grams or 121.3493 grains.}$$

Estimation of Projectile Velocity

The capacity of an existing cartridge design to propel an existing or conceptual projectile composed of an exotic alloy or material to its maximum velocity may be approximated by treating the force produced by the expansion of the propellant gases upon the bullet as a momentum transaction. Since force imparts over time, a change in momentum of the projectile,

$$F = m(\Delta v/\Delta t) = \Delta p/\Delta t,$$

the impulse produced by the existing design is the basis for this approximation. It must, however, be borne in mind that this relationship relies upon the assumed availability and employment of an optimal, or closely equivalent, propellant within the functional constraints of an existing cartridge design. This process also requires that the respective impulse of the existing and conceptual projectiles be treated as being equivalent to one another.

The approximation is affected by using Newton's third law of motion,

$$m_1 v_1 = m_2 v_2,$$

which must then be rearranged to determine the maximum attainable velocity (v_2) of the existing or conceptual exotic projectile design,

$$[(m_1 \times v_1) \div m_2] = v_2.$$

Using the .45-caliber, zinc-alloy, hollow point projectile weighing 121.3493 grains from the prior example, and the ability of the .45 ACP cartridge to propel a .45-caliber, 185-grain, jacketed hollow point projectile to a velocity of 950 feet per second, the estimated maximum attainable velocity of the zinc-alloy projectile, using an appropriate propellant would be:

$$[(185 \times 950) \div 121.3493] = 1,448.2984 \text{ feet per second.}$$

Once the required input variables have been estimated, the model may then be used to predict the terminal ballistic performance of the exotic projectile.

Examples

The following examples illustrate the application of the model to expanding and non-expanding exotic projectile designs.

<u>Example #1</u>

A .45-caliber, hollow point bullet (initial diameter = 0.4515 inch) composed of zinc alloy and weighing 121 grains is fired at a velocity of 1,450 feet per second (441.96 meters per second) through a light-weight clothing barrier into a water test medium. The projectile expands radically, losing forty-three percent of its weight, and is subsequently recovered as a short cylinder that has a diameter of 0.4515 inch (11.4681 millimeters or 1.14681 centimeters) and a retained mass of 69 grains (4.4711 grams). To what depth would it penetrate in soft tissue that has a density of 1,040 ± 20 kg/m^3?

First, determine the value of the uniaxial strain proportionality, ϵ:

$$\epsilon = {}^3\sqrt{D_{mm}} \times \sqrt{(\sigma_t \div \rho_t)}$$

35

$$\epsilon = \sqrt[3]{11.4681} \times \sqrt{(1,000,000 \div 1,040)}$$

$$\epsilon = \sqrt[3]{11.4681} \times \sqrt{(961.538462)}$$

$$\epsilon = 2.2551 \times 31.008684$$

$$\epsilon = 69.9277.$$

Using the calculated value for ϵ, predict the maximum penetration depth of the 69-grain (4.4711 grams) cylinder in soft tissue that has a density of 1.040 grams per cubic centimeter:

$$S = LN [(V_i \div \epsilon)^2 + 1] \times [M \div (\pi \times (\tfrac{1}{2}D_{cm})^2 \times \rho \times C_D)]$$

$$S = LN [(441.96 \div 69.9277)^2 + 1] \times [4.4711 \div (3.1415927 \times (\tfrac{1}{2} \times 1.14681)^2 \times 1.040 \times 0.833333)]$$

$$S = LN [(6.3202)^2 + 1] \times [4.4711 \div (0.895209)]$$

$$S = LN [40.9449] \times [4.9945]$$

$$S = [3.7122] \times [4.9945]$$

$$S = 18.5406 \text{ centimeters or } 7.2994 \text{ inches.}$$

Assuming that the .45-caliber, hollow point bullet was fired into an abdomen having a finite thickness (T_F) of 10.00 inches (25.40 centimeters) and that the cylinder remaining after the projectile's radical expansion does not exit the opposite side of the abdomen, what would be the total mass of the permanent wound cavity (M_{PC})

produced by the expanded bullet remaining inside of the abdomen?

Determine the mass within the permanent wound cavity (M_{PC}) produced by the bullet's passage:

$$M_{PC} = \Pi \times (\tfrac{1}{2}D_{cm})^2 \times S \times \rho \times \Phi$$

$$M_{PC} = 3.1415927 \times (\tfrac{1}{2} \times 1.14681)^2$$
$$\times\ 18.5406 \times 1.040 \times 1.000$$

$$M_{PC} = 3.1415927 \times 0.3288 \times 18.5406 \times 1.040 \times 1.000$$

$$M_{PC} = 19.9177 \text{ grams or } 0.7026 \text{ ounce.}$$

Example #2

Predict the maximum penetration depth in soft tissue ($\rho = 1{,}040 \pm 20 \text{ kg/m}^3$) of a non-deforming, 67-grain, .40-caliber bullet (10.1600 millimeters or 1.0160 centimeters) having a full metal jacket truncated cone (FMJTC) configuration that is constructed of a "gilding metal" full metal jacket filled with a solid, high-strength, epoxy core. Assume that the bullet has an impact velocity of 1,870 feet per second (569.976 meters per second) and a recovered weight of 67 grains (4.3415 grams).

First, determine the value of the uniaxial strain proportionality, ϵ:

$$\epsilon = \sqrt[3]{D_{mm}} \times \sqrt{(\sigma_t \div \rho_t)}$$

$$\epsilon = \sqrt[3]{10.1600} \times \sqrt{(1{,}000{,}000 \div 1{,}040)}$$

$$\epsilon = \sqrt[3]{10.1600} \times \sqrt{(961.538462)}$$

$$\epsilon = 2.165864266 \times 31.008684$$

$$\epsilon = 67.1606.$$

Using the calculated value for ϵ, predict the maximum penetration depth of the undeformed, .40-caliber, full metal jacket truncated cone bullet, weighing 67 grains (4.3415 grams) and having an impact velocity of 1,870 feet per second (569.976 meters per second), in soft tissue that has a density of 1.040 grams per cubic centimeter:

$$S = LN \, [(V_i \div \epsilon)^2 + 1] \times [M \div (\pi \times (\tfrac{1}{2}D_{cm})^2 \times \rho \times C_D)]$$

$$S = LN \, [(569.976 \div 67.1606)^2 + 1] \times [4.3415 \div (3.1415927 \times (\tfrac{1}{2} \times 1.0160)^2 \times 1.040 \times 0.551937)]$$

$$S = LN \, [(8.4868)^2 + 1] \times [4.3415 \div (0.4654)]$$

$$S = LN \, [73.0258] \times [9.3285]$$

$$S = [4.2908] \times [9.3285]$$

$$S = 40.0267 \text{ centimeters or } 15.7585 \text{ inches.}$$

At what velocity would the undeformed, .40-caliber, FMJTC bullet, weighing 67 grains (4.3415 grams), exit the opposite side of an abdomen having a thickness (T_F) of 12.00 inches (30.48 centimeters)?

First, determine the value of "x":

$$x = (S - T_F) \div [M \div (\pi \times (\tfrac{1}{2}D_{cm})^2 \times \rho \times C_D)]$$

$$x = (40.0267 - 30.48) \div [4.3415 \div (3.1415927 \times (\tfrac{1}{2} \times 1.0160)^2 \times 1.040 \times 0.551937)]$$

$$x = (9.5467) \div [4.3415 \div (0.4654)]$$

$$x = (9.5467) \div [9.3285]$$

$$x = 1.0234.$$

Next, predict the residual (exit) velocity of the .40-caliber, FMJTC bullet by substituting the value 1.0234 for "x" in the following equation:

$$V_{rx} = \epsilon \times \sqrt{(e^x - 1)}$$

$$V_{rx} = 67.1606 \times \sqrt{(2.7182818285^{\,1.0234} - 1)}$$

$$V_{rx} = 67.1606 \times \sqrt{(2.7826 - 1)}$$

$$V_{rx} = 67.1606 \times \sqrt{(1.7826)}$$

$$V_{rx} = 67.1606 \times 1.3351$$

$$V_{rx} = 89.6661 \text{ meters per second or } 294.1801 \text{ feet per second.}$$

As demonstrated by the prior examples, the terminal ballistic performance of projectiles of exotic composition and unconventional design may be predicted using mathematical modeling.

While certain terminal ballistic performance parameters such as expanded diameter and retained mass may only be obtained through actual testing in shear-validated 10-percent ordnance gelatin or water, the model allows speculative investigation of conceptual designs and their potential performance prior to fabrication.

Because a readily available means of testing projectiles is to the benefit of the armed professional, the process for constructing a practical, yet durable, test fixture is addressed in the next chapter.

6

A Practical Test Method

When compared to the logistic and technical difficulties inherent in the employment of shear-validated 10-percent ordnance gelatin as a tissue simulant, the practical utility, logistic convenience, and relative insensitivity of water to ambient environmental conditions should make the employment of water as a tissue simulant an attractive, cost-effective option to the armed professional. The value of these benefits is difficult to deny.

Test Fixture Construction

The construction of a fixture suitable for testing projectiles in water is simple and very inexpensive (the total materials cost including enough plastic bags for several tests is about $40.00 - $60.00) and can be completed in less than ninety minutes.

Although several design variations are possible, the most practical and durable design for a test fixture is that of a semi-circular trough constructed from an eight-foot section of eight-inch diameter, PVC Schedule 40 pipe which may be constructed using the following materials and equipment:

1. an eight-foot length of PVC Schedule 40 pipe, eight inches in diameter;
2. an eight-foot length of four-by-four-inch lumber;
3. two rolls of duct tape;
4. a saw suitable for cutting PVC pipe and wood; and,
5. a pair of scissors or a sharp knife.

Once the necessary equipment and materials have been acquired, the fabrication process is easy to complete.

The eight-foot length of eight-inch diameter PVC pipe may, for the sake of portability, be cut to a length of six feet (seventy-two inches) or left at its original length as purchased. Once the PVC pipe has been cut to the desired length, it must then be cut in half lengthwise so that two half-pipes (or troughs) are produced, one of which will be used for the construction of the test fixture. The other half may be used to construct another test fixture that can either be coupled together with the first trough for testing and recovering non-expanding projectile designs or given to a friend interested in conducting his own tests.

After cutting the PVC pipe in half lengthwise, remove any burrs or sharp fragments from the freshly cut edges of the PVC trough and wrap at least one layer of duct tape over the entire length of the PVC trough using a slightly overlapping spiral pattern. This should serve to reinforce the trough against the mechanical forces exerted by the rupture of the water bags (during the more dynamic tests) used to contain the water test medium.

The eight-foot length of four-by-four-inch lumber should then be cut into two lengths of approximately four feet each. These sections of lumber will have enough mass to stabilize the PVC trough against rolling or other unwanted movement on uneven surfaces when placed lengthwise along both sides of the PVC trough while remaining light enough to transport easily.

After the construction of the test fixture has been completed, testing may be conducted by obtaining several boxes of generic-brand, gallon-size, sealable plastic storage bags, and filling them completely with water. When sealing the bags, care should be taken to ensure that little or no air remains inside them. The bags must then be arranged, one next to another, along the trough's length forming a horizontal water column. Setting the bags upright and sideways (along their widest dimension) in the trough allows the most efficient use of the bags. Care must also be taken to align the bags to ensure that the bags remain positioned properly during testing.

Almost any imaginable intermediate barrier (within reason) may be placed in front of the horizontal water column so long as care is taken to ensure that the projectile being fired through the barrier and into the water column is directed parallel, and as closely as possible, to the central axis running the length of the horizontal water column. If the projectile's trajectory is misaligned to any great extent, it may exit the side of the horizontal water column before coming to rest in the test fixture. This will prevent recovery of the projectile and require retesting in order to evaluate the projectile's performance.

Where a more disposable or convenient alternative to the use of the half-pipe test fixture described above is desired, a suitable number of half-gallon, paper-board beverage cartons (such as those used for milk or orange juice) may be filled with water and carefully aligned in a row on a flat surface. Where no such surface is available, the cartons may be situated upon a narrow piece of plywood or a rigid plastic sheet. The half-gallon cartons measure about 3.75 inches on a side (and about nine inches in height), so most tests of expanding projectile designs should require the use of no more than twelve cartons. Set upright and aligned carefully, they should provide approximately forty-five inches of usable water column for testing.

In researching the suitability of the half-gallon paper-board cartons for ballistic testing, it was discovered that the light-weight paper-board material used in the construction of the cartons has little, if any, effect upon the terminal ballistic performance of expanding test projectiles.

Test Barriers

Although a projectile design may be tested without the presence of any sort of intermediate barrier, the inclusion of barriers commonly encountered in one's environment is a valid method for assessing the effect of those materials upon the terminal ballistic performance of the projectile. Only actual testing will reveal unexpected or problematic performance traits that may be of concern to the armed professional.

Modern hollow point ammunition requires the entry of a fluid or hydrocolloidal medium into its expansion cavity to produce the hydraulic forces necessary to drive expansion. As projectiles pass through a barrier, their expansion cavities may become deformed or obstructed by any material that they pass through (especially in the case of hollow point ammunition) and offer altered, or even unacceptable terminal ballistic performance. For example, if a jacketed hollow point bullet passes through sheet metal (like that found in automotive construction), it may "rivet" (the bullet's lead core moves forward and distorts the bullet's jacket under the stress of penetrating the sheet metal) during its passage through the barrier. It is also possible that the bullet could lose some of its initial mass through an ablative mechanism, adversely affecting its terminal ballistic performance or reducing its depth of penetration more than might be expected or desired.

If a valid test barrier is sought, the armed professional should consider the physical obstacles and types of clothing commonly encountered in his environment. Ideally, the materials should be implemented as test barriers based upon the probability of having to shoot through them during a lethal-force incident.

If the determination of an environmentally common barrier is not possible, or if the alternatives are too numerous to narrow down, the use of a heavy-clothing barrier consisting of four layers of sixteen-ounce denim is an inexpensive and easily repeatable "failure test" that should adequately test the mechanical performance of any premium, expanding projectile design. Such testing is necessary because dense, fibrous fabric and other materials can enter, accumulate within, and possibly obstruct the jacketed hollow point bullet's expansion cavity and reduce or prevent the expansion of the bullet.

Other barrier materials common across a broad range of environments and suitable for use as a test barrier are automotive sheet-metal panels (usually 20-gauge, cold-rolled, mild steel sheet approximately one millimeter thick), automotive glass, light- and middle-weight fabrics, sheetrock, and plywood panels. Only testing will reveal the unexpected or adverse effect of a barrier material upon the terminal ballistic performance of a projectile.

Measurement of Impact Velocity

One of the input variables necessary for the evaluation of ammunition being tested in water is the velocity of the bullet at the instant of impact.

The first and most preferable method for obtaining this parameter is through direct measurement. This method requires the placement of a chronograph (an electronic device that measures the velocity of a passing projectile) a few feet in front of the impact face of the test fixture in order to measure the actual velocity of the test projectile prior to impact. The limitation of such a technique is that, should the test result in a particularly violent impact, water could find its way into the chronograph and damage it. It is possible to protect the device by wrapping it in plastic, leaving only the detection ports exposed, but the risk of serious damage remains.

The second and next most preferable method of determining a projectile's impact velocity is that of firing ten or more test projectiles over a chronograph in order to obtain an average velocity. The average of the sample population (*n*) is then used as the impact velocity for the purpose of evaluating the projectile's terminal performance. The difference in "actual" versus "average" impact velocities produced by high quality, self-defense ammunition is usually small enough to have no significant effect upon the results generated by the model. This method also has the benefit of allowing the determination of a projectile's impact velocity at another time and place of greater convenience without the risk of adding water to the insides of a valuable electronic instrument.

The third and least preferable method for determining the impact velocity of a test projectile is the use of the ammunition manufacturer's advertised velocity. This method amounts to nothing more than speculation because there is no way to confirm that the projectile actually attains the advertised velocity. Because ammunition is loaded according to strict industry-specified pressure levels, the velocity produced by any ammunition can vary widely among handguns depending upon manufacturing tolerances. Because of this, there is no guarantee that a certain firearm bore will produce the advertised velocity claimed by the ammunition manufacturer. Not knowing the velocity at which a projectile strikes the test medium introduces significant error into the evaluative process and will, more likely than not, yield an inaccurate prediction of the projectile's potential terminal ballistic performance.

Test Projectile Recovery and Measurement

Once a projectile has been fired into the test fixture and come to rest, it must be recovered, weighed, and its average diameter determined.

Typically, an expanding projectile design will be recovered one quarter to a little more than one-half of the way down the length of the test fixture. If an expanding design (such as a JHP) is not recovered because it passed through the entire length of the horizontal water column (seventy-two to ninety-six inches), it is most likely the result of the projectile's failure to expand. This means that it will behave as a non-expanding configuration of the same weight and produce enough penetration to exit the rear of the test fixture.

In order to determine the correct weight of the recovered projectile, it must be cleaned of any barrier material that has become attached to it, dried of water, and weighed on an accurate scale. To be used in the model, the weight of the projectile must be expressed in grams. If a reloading scale such as that used by those who reload their own ammunition is used to weigh the recovered projectile (such scales usually provide their measurements in grains, an avoirdupois unit of measurement that is equal to $1/7,000^{th}$ of a pound), then the proper conversion factor must be used to convert the measurement from grains to grams. In order to make the conversion to grams, multiply the (recovered) projectile weight in grains by 0.06479891.

After weighing, a determination of the projectile's average expanded diameter must be made. This process requires the use of a Vernier caliper capable of making measurements to the nearest thousandth of an inch. An equal number of measurements across the largest and smallest widths of the recovered projectile's expansion face should be added together and then divided by the total number of measurements taken to yield the average expanded diameter of the recovered bullet. It is also necessary to convert the average expanded diameter of the recovered bullet to centimeters (multiply by 2.54) for use in the quantitative model's primary mathematical argument and to millimeters (multiply by 25.4) for use in the quantitative model's governing expression.

Test Population Size

The number of times that a specific projectile design is subjected to a single test parameter is dependent upon the armed professional's budget and how much effort the armed professional wishes to invest in evaluating a specific projectile design.

Multiple tests of a single projectile design result in an increased probability of detecting a defect or deficiency in the design. Because it would be tremendously impractical and time-consuming to test an entire box of ammunition, a more reasonable alternative would be to test three to five randomly selected sample projectiles. Ultimately, the validity of any evaluative procedure rests upon its proper implementation and a departure from an acceptable sample size will probably result in an incomplete or inaccurate assessment of a projectile's capabilities.

7

Myths and Misconceptions

Without an understanding of the physics of the ballistic wounding mechanism, it is difficult to establish an accurate representation of the relationship that exists between the ballistic wounding mechanism and physical incapacitation. In the past, several implausible and misguided constructs intended to qualify and quantify the terminal ballistic performance of self-defense ammunition have been offered and will be dispelled in this chapter.

"Knockdown Power"

The idea that a projectile, fired from a handgun at any realistic velocity, can involuntarily knock a person to the ground or propel a person rearward over a significant distance upon impact violates Newton's third law of motion. The fallacy of such an assertion is easily demonstrated.

As discussed in the second chapter, Newton's third law of motion prescribes that, "To every action there is an equal and opposite reaction", and is expressed by the equation,

$$mv = mv,$$

which is also known as the law of conservation of momentum. Proponents of this type of assertion ignore the fact that the law of conservation of momentum mandates that the product of one side of the equation must equal the product of the other.

For example, many have seen a character in a motion picture take a full charge of buckshot to the

49

chest from a shotgun at close range. Upon impact, the character is propelled rearward several feet through a nearby plate-glass window or other barrier. While such a depiction is certainly entertaining, it fails to stand upon examination of what must actually occur according to Newton's third law of motion. The analysis of this example is simple to conduct and is carried out for the sake of ensuring an understanding of the momentum transaction that would actually take place.

In order to establish the constraints of this analysis, assume that the character being shot weighs 185 pounds (his mass, now defined as m_2, is equal to 83.91 kilograms) and that he absorbs the entire load of 00-buckshot into his chest as fired from the shotgun at a range of six inches. This condition minimizes the velocity lost by the 00-buckshot pellets as they travel from the shotgun's muzzle and strike the character's chest. Let it also be assumed for the sake of this analysis, that the shotgun being fired into the character's chest is chambered to fire 12-gauge ammunition and that the charge consists of a magnum payload of fifteen 00-buckshot pellets. Each pellet has a nominal mass of 3.486 grams (for a total mass of 52.29 grams, now defined as m_1), an impact velocity of 1,225 feet per second (373.38 meters per second, now defined as v_1), and all fifteen buckshot are assumed to strike and remain within the character's chest after impact making his total mass 83.96229 kilograms.

The character's rearward velocity may then be determined by rearranging the equation

$$m_1 \times v_1 = m_2 \times v_2$$

to solve for the character's acquired rearward velocity, v_2, so that

$$(m_1 \times v_1) \div (m_1 + m_2) = v_2.$$

Then, the appropriate numerical values are substituted in order to calculate the character's rearward velocity, v_2, upon impact so that

$$(0.05229 \text{ kg} \times 373.38 \text{ mps}) \div (83.96229 \text{ kg}) = v_2$$

$$(19.524 \text{ kg·mps}) \div (83.96229 \text{ kg}) = v_2$$

$$v_2 = 0.2325 \text{ mps.}$$

The character's rearward velocity of 0.2325 meters per second is equivalent to a velocity of about nine inches per second. This means that the maximum distance that the 185-pound character could be picked up and thrown rearward by such an impact is less than a centimeter if frictional effects are ignored.

For handgun projectiles having much less momentum, the implication is quite clear; no one can be knocked down or picked up and thrown rearward any appreciable distance solely by the impact of a handgun projectile at any reasonably attainable velocity.

"Energy Deposit"

Contrary to the proven tenets of thermodynamics, the "energy-deposit", or "energy-dump" hypothesis asserts that the kinetic energy possessed by a high-velocity (in excess of 1,300 feet per second) handgun projectile can contribute to, and even significantly increase, the magnitude of the ballistic wounding mechanism through a thermal effect. As demonstrated by example in the second chapter, even the amount of kinetic energy possessed by a large-caliber rifle projectile at supersonic velocity is of insufficient magnitude to damage soft tissue through a thermodynamic mechanism.

In addition to the thermodynamic effects alleged by those advocating the use of light-weight handgun projectiles at supersonic velocities is the assertion that the increased magnitude of the temporary cavity produced by the passage of such a projectile will significantly increase the efficacy of the ballistic wounding mechanism through the greater radial displacement of soft tissue away from the projectile's path. While it can certainly be argued that an increase in the magnitude of the temporary cavity might result in additional permanent damage to susceptible tissues surrounding the projectile's path, the potential of this effect is mitigated by the fact that most of the tissues impinged upon by such a projectile will likely have tensile- and compressive-yield strengths superior to the forces to which they are subjected. Therefore, the effect of temporary cavitation produced by handgun projectiles is not reliable enough to warrant consideration as a significant ballistic wounding mechanism.

As past independent experimentation and experience have demonstrated, driving a projectile to an extremely high velocity (often well above the projectile's design limit) in the pursuit of improving terminal ballistic performance is likely to result in an increased rate of fragmentation of the projectile. More often than not, the significant loss of projectile mass leads to greatly diminished terminal penetration and a corresponding reduction of the permanent wound cavity volume and damaged soft tissue mass therein.

"Stopping Power"

The concept of "stopping power" constitutes a simple way to look at the very complex interaction of a projectile striking and passing through a human body. The concept broadly encompasses multiple facets of physics, anatomy, and physiology in an attempt to package them into an over-simplified, "made-to-sell" answer.

The term "power", when used in the context of the discipline of physics, is defined as the ability of a force to do a specific amount of work upon an object within a specific period of time. It has nothing whatsoever to do with the concept of power as used within the colloquial term "stopping power". This important distinction is a significant source of confusion for many because those lacking a technical education are inclined to perceive it as a valid application of the concept of power as it pertains to physics, even though it possesses no such quality when used in the vernacular. Not surprisingly, the misuse of such terminology continues to promote confusion and misunderstanding where the discussion of terminal ballistic performance is concerned.

The colloquial use of the term "power" when used in the context of "stopping power" is a semantic abuse of a technical term that also seems to carry with it the notion that every other aspect of terminal ballistic performance (shot placement, assailant anatomy, impact velocity, projectile expansion, terminal penetration, and retained projectile mass) may be taken for granted or simply ignored.

Consider the mathematical model for "relative stopping power" described in *Textbook of Pistols and Revolvers: Their Ammunition, Ballistics, and Use*, written by General Julian S. Hatcher in 1935, and cited by many as a means of quantifying the "relative stopping power" (or RSP) of handgun projectiles:

$$RSP = k \times B \times M \times V \times A$$

Hatcher's RSP formula is a contrived mathematical arrangement in which a projectile's momentum, MV, is multiplied by the projectile's cross-sectional area, A, a dimensionless bullet-shape factor, B, and a scaling constant, k. The product of Hatcher's RSP formula suggests that the unitary quantification of "relative stopping power" is correctly expressed in either pound · feet per second · inch^2 or kilogram · meter per second · meter^2. Despite this suggestion, the unitary product (a projectile's momentum multiplied by its cross-sectional area, a dimensionless bullet-shape factor and a scaling constant) of this contrived mathematical arrangement is not an expression of power in any sense of the term.

When projectiles of identical design are evaluated using Hatcher's RSP formula, a .45-caliber, 230-grain, full metal jacket round nose bullet having a velocity of 870 feet per second (RSP = 64.01), is claimed to be capable of producing more than two and one half times the "relative stopping power" of a 9-millimeter, 115-grain, full metal jacket round nose bullet having a velocity of 1,120 feet per second (RSP = 25.38). Even though both projectiles produce permanent wound cavities that are proportional to their respective diameters over virtually identical penetration depths (26.03 and 26.04 inches, respectively), Hatcher's formula assigns a "relative stopping power" value to the .45-caliber projectile that is disproportionate to the magnitude of actual tissue damage that it produces. While the .45-caliber projectile would permanently damage 62.4 percent more tissue than the 9-millimeter projectile would over the same penetration depth, the magnitude of the .45-caliber projectile's "relative stopping power" is stated by Hatcher's RSP formula to be 2.52 times greater than that which would be produced by the 9-millimeter bullet, even though both of the projectiles produce physical trauma through the same mechanism: tissue permanently damaged through direct contact with the projectile.

Statistical Analysis of Combat Data

The numerous material difficulties associated with the concept of "stopping power" has not prevented the collection and interpretation of combat data from the field as a means of quantifying "stopping power". Composed of citizen and police shootings, combat data has been converted into arbitrarily defined percentile rankings that are meant to convey the relative "effectiveness" of self-defense ammunition. The problem with such a dimensionless approach is that it ignores every other possible aspect of terminal ballistic performance involved in the production of incapacitation. Attempting to quantify the "stopping power" of ammunition based solely upon its mass and (potential) velocity while implicitly assuming that suitable terminal ballistic performance (projectile expansion, retained mass, penetration depth, permanent wound cavity volume, and permanent wound mass) will occur, is an unsound and dangerous practice.

Such faulty statistical methodology fails to consider the inevitable and nearly infinite anatomical variances that exist within any population, rendering impossible the precise duplication of identical tissue damage even when projectiles of the same configuration, diameter, mass, and velocity are considered. Ignoring the highly variable nature of human anatomy condemns the concept of statistically based "stopping power" to failure. As a result, until it is properly defined, the term "stopping power" cannot be used as a basis upon which to establish any meaningful quantification or qualification of the ballistic wounding mechanism and its effects.

The greatest problem inherent in statistical approaches is that every shooting incident is a separate and independent event that is related to no other. Every incident in which shots are fired that strike an assailant who is engaging in lethal violence has a binary outcome that cannot be predicted by an arbitrarily defined success rate that has been derived from the statistical analysis of the ammunition's prior performance. Either an assailant's life-threatening assault is terminated by the irresistible effects of the ballistic wounding mechanism or the assailant persists in his life-threatening assault because he has not been subjected to conditions sufficient to produce involuntary incapacitation.

Simply put, arbitrarily defined physiological incapacitation response criteria and success rates or percentages generated from the statistical analyses of prior armed engagements cannot be used to predict the outcome of future armed engagements where an assailant is struck by one or more projectiles. It is also in serious error to assign dimensionless values obtained from a contrived formula to a specific brand or type of ammunition and assume that similar performance will result in any other shooting irrespective of the inestimable dynamics that comprise these completely independent and tremendously complex events.

8

Barrier Effects

Where shots are fired in order to neutralize an armed assailant who is engaged in (or about to engage in) life-threatening violence, the projectiles will almost invariably have to pass through and defeat some sort of intermediate barrier before striking the armed assailant. The most commonly encountered intermediate barrier, the clothing and outerwear (of various weights and qualities) worn by an armed assailant, can obstruct the expansion cavity of an expanding projectile design with tough, fibrous material and cause it to fail to expand as it traverses soft tissue. Other barrier materials can have an adverse effect upon the terminal performance of a projectile and, in extreme cases, even prevent it from reaching its intended target.

Heavy Clothing

Because armed professionals visiting or inhabiting the northern latitudes of the United States will encounter climatic variations that will cause considerable fluctuation in the weight of clothing being worn by potential aggressors, it is to the benefit of the armed professional to have at least a cursory understanding of how this variable can influence the terminal ballistic performance of self-defense ammunition.

The penetration of skin or clothing by a projectile, unlike shear-validated 10-percent ordnance gelatin, is a transaction that is best described by using an energy relationship that relies upon the projectile's impact velocity, mass, cross-sectional area, and the total areal density of the garment(s) and skin. These variables are used to establish the ballistic limit (V_{50}) of a specified total garment weight and skin thickness and may be used to predict the residual (remaining) velocity of a projectile after it has defeated a skin and clothing barrier.

The relationship is insensitive to the nose configuration of both expanding (JHPs) and non-expanding (FMJs, wadcutters, etc.) projectiles and is accurately quantified by the mathematical model described in the reference source, "Estimating Ballistic Limits of Skin and Clothing for Projectiles".

The power law for evaluating the effect of garment weight and skin thickness upon transient projectile velocity correlates highly against experimental data and is expressed in the equation

$$V_{50} = 309.13 \times [(2M) \div (\pi \times (\tfrac{1}{2}D)^2 \times \rho \times T)]^{-0.38708},$$

where M is the mass of the projectile in grams, D is the diameter of the projectile in centimeters, ρ is the density of skin in grams per cubic centimeter (about 1.060 grams per centimeter^3), and T is the total combined areal density (a function of thickness) of the textile barrier in grams per centimeter^2.

Once determined, the ballistic limit (V_{50}) and the projectile's impact velocity (V_i) may be used to predict the residual velocity (V_r) of the projectile after it defeats a skin or textile barrier by employing the energy relationship described by the equation

$$V_r = \sqrt{[V_i^2 - V_{50}^2]}.$$

Where a projectile's terminal ballistic performance in soft tissue is to be evaluated after it has passed through a garment, skin, or a combination of garment(s) and skin, the projectile's residual velocity (V_r) must be used as its impact velocity (V_i) in the quantitative terminal ballistic performance model.

Since garments are typically incapable of sustaining the hydraulic forces necessary to initiate and drive the expansion of transient, expanding projectile designs, expanding projectiles must be evaluated as non-expanding designs using the textile penetration model. Where an expanding projectile design traverses soft tissue after a textile barrier has been defeated, it must be evaluated as having the potential for expansion.

The following example illustrates the application of the model to non-expanding (and expanding) projectile designs.

Example

Determine the ballistic limit (V_{50}) of a .45-caliber (1.14681 centimeter), full metal jacket round nose bullet, weighing 230 grains (14.9038 grams) which must pass through a heavy winter coat, a heavy sweater, and a thermal undershirt that have a total areal density of 32 ounces per square foot (about 0.9765 grams/ centimeter^2):

$$V_{50} = 309.13 \times [(2M) \div (\pi \times (\tfrac{1}{2}D)^2 \times \rho \times T)]^{-0.38708}$$

$$V_{50} = 309.13 \times [(2 \times 14.9038) \div (\pi \times (\tfrac{1}{2} \times 1.14681)^2 \times 1.000 \times 0.9765)]^{-0.38708}$$

$$V_{50} = 309.13 \times [(29.8076) \div (\pi \times (0.573405)^2 \times 0.9765)]^{-0.38708}$$

$$V_{50} = 309.13 \times [(29.8076) \div (1.0087)]^{-0.38708}$$

$$V_{50} = 309.13 \times [29.5511]^{-0.38708}$$

$$V_{50} = 309.13 \times 0.2696$$

$$V_{50} = 83.3414 \text{ meters per second}$$
$$(273.4298 \text{ feet per second}).$$

Using the ballistic limit obtained above (V_{50} = 83.3414 meters per second), predict the residual velocity (V_r) of the .45-caliber, 230-grain, FMJRN bullet after it passes through the garments by employing the energy relationship described earlier:

$$V_r = \sqrt{[V_i^2 - V_{50}^2]}$$

$$V_r = \sqrt{[(259.08)^2 - (83.3414)^2]}$$

$$V_r = \sqrt{[(67,122.4464) - (6,945.7889)]}$$

$$V_r = \sqrt{[60,176.6575]}$$

$$V_r = 245.3093 \text{ meters per second}$$
$$(804.8205 \text{ feet per second}).$$

Using the residual velocity of 804.8205 feet per second (245.3093 meters per second), predict the maximum terminal penetration of the .45-caliber (11.4681 millimeters), 230-grain, FMJRN bullet in soft tissue (ρ = 1,040 ± 20 kg/m^3) after it passes through the garments.

First, determine the value of the uniaxial strain proportionality, ϵ:

$$\epsilon = \sqrt[3]{D_{mm}} \times \sqrt{(\sigma_t \div \rho_t)}$$

$$\epsilon = \sqrt[3]{11.4681} \times \sqrt{(1{,}000{,}000 \div 1{,}040)}$$

$$\epsilon = \sqrt[3]{11.4681} \times \sqrt{(961.538462)}$$

$$\epsilon = 2.2551 \times 31.008684$$

$$\epsilon = 69.9277.$$

Using the calculated value for ϵ, predict the maximum penetration depth of the .45-caliber, 230-grain (14.9038 grams), FMJRN bullet, having an impact (residual) velocity of 804.8205 feet per second (245.3093 meters per second), in soft tissue that has a density of 1.040 grams per cubic centimeter:

$$S = LN\,[(V_r \div \epsilon)^2 + 1] \times [M \div (\pi \times (\tfrac{1}{2}D_{cm})^2 \times \rho \times C_D)]$$

$$S = LN\,[(245.3093 \div 69.9277)^2 + 1] \times [14.9038 \div (3.1415927 \times (\tfrac{1}{2} \times 1.14681)^2 \times 1.040 \times 0.573576)]$$

$$S = LN\,[(3.5080)^2 + 1] \times [14.9038 \div (0.6162)]$$

$$S = LN\,[13.3061] \times [24.1866]$$

$$S = 2.5882 \times 24.1866$$

$$S = 62.5998 \text{ centimeters or } 24.6456 \text{ inches.}$$

As illustrated in the example provided above, even heavy clothing has little effect upon the terminal ballistic performance of large-diameter projectiles moving at subsonic velocities. After defeating heavy clothing, the velocity loss (about 45.20 feet per second) constitutes only about 5.3 percent of the projectile's initial velocity and represents a loss of about 10.35 percent of the projectile's initial kinetic energy. As a result, the .45-caliber, 230-grain, FMJRN projectile remains capable of producing more than 24 inches of penetration in soft tissue even after defeating heavy clothing. Because expansion cavities in expanding projectile designs can become obstructed with dense, fibrous material and fail to expand in soft tissue after passing through heavy garments, it is entirely possible for a jacketed hollow point projectile to demonstrate penetration similar to that of a non-expanding, full metal jacket projectile under such conditions.

Cold-Rolled Steel Sheet

In order to neutralize a lethal threat, the armed professional may be required to fire through the cold-rolled mild steel sheet that is commonly found in automotive construction, office furniture, and other frequently encountered objects. Although such occurrences are relatively uncommon, it is to the advantage of the armed professional to have an understanding of the terminal ballistic performance of projectiles that must pass through cold-rolled mild steel sheet prior to striking an armed assailant.

A mathematical model based upon the minimum energy required to penetrate cold-rolled mild steel sheet was developed using data produced by .25-caliber, 9-millimeter, .40-caliber, and .45-caliber test projectiles that struck, and in most cases penetrated, twenty-four cold-rolled AISI 1006 mild steel sheets of varying thickness. The 11-, 16-, and 20-gauge, cold-rolled AISI 1006 mild steel sheets, measuring 12" x 36" and having an average Brinell hardness number (BHN) of 100, were struck by jacketed hollow point and full metal jacket round nose projectiles at subsonic and supersonic velocities. Chronographs, placed immediately before and after each cold-rolled mild steel test sheet, recorded the impact velocity and residual velocity of each test projectile.

The test data was fitted to a modified DeMarre armor penetration equation,

$$T = KD \times (MV^2 \div D^3)^{0.800},$$

that relies upon the minimum kinetic energy required, expressed by the term $(MV^2 \div D^3)$, to penetrate a specific thickness of cold-rolled mild steel sheet where $K = 9.35 \times 10^{-9}$, T is the maximum sheet thickness (in inches) that can be penetrated by the projectile, M is the mass of the projectile (in grains), V is the impact velocity of the projectile (in feet per second), and D is the diameter of the projectile (in inches). When evaluated against 108 data points, the modified DeMarre armor penetration equation accurately predicts the terminal penetration (T), ballistic limit (V_{50}), and residual velocity (V_r) of service-caliber projectiles against cold-rolled AISI 1006 mild steel sheet with a margin of error of 2.35 percent and exhibits a correlation of $r = +0.981$.

The modified DeMarre armor penetration equation may be rearranged to solve for and calculate the ballistic limit, V_{50} (in feet per second), of any thickness of cold-rolled mild steel sheet

$$V_{50} = \sqrt{[(D^3 \div M) \times (T \div KD)^{1.250}]},$$

where T is the thickness (in inches) of the cold-rolled mild steel sheet to be penetrated, D is the diameter of the projectile (in inches), and M is the mass of the projectile (in grains).

Once the ballistic limit (V_{50}) of a projectile has been determined, it may be used with the projectile's impact velocity (V_i) to predict the residual velocity (V_r) of the projectile after it penetrates a cold-rolled mild steel sheet by employing the energy relationship described by the equation

$$V_r = \sqrt{[V_i^2 - V_{50}^2]}.$$

Where a projectile's terminal ballistic performance in soft tissue is to be assessed after it has passed through a cold-rolled mild steel sheet, the projectile's residual velocity (V_r) must be used as its impact velocity (V_i) in the quantitative terminal ballistic performance model.

The following example illustrates the application of the modified DeMarre armor penetration equation to typical service-caliber projectiles.

Example

Determine the maximum thickness of cold-rolled AISI 1006 mild steel sheet that a 9-millimeter (0.355 inch) full metal jacket round nose bullet, weighing 115 grains and having an impact velocity of 1,175 feet per second, can successfully penetrate:

$$T = KD \times (MV^2 \div D^3)^{0.800}$$

$$T = 9.35 \times 10^{-9} \times 0.355 \times ((115 \times 1{,}175^2) \div 0.355^3)^{0.800}$$

$$T = 3.31925 \times 10^{-9} \times ((115 \times 1{,}380{,}625) \div 0.044738875)^{0.800}$$

$$T = 3.31925 \times 10^{-9} \times 43{,}658{,}701.1757$$

$$T = 0.144914 \text{ inch } (3.6808 \text{ millimeters}).$$

Given a 9-millimeter (0.355 inch), full metal jacket round nose bullet weighing 115 grains, determine the ballistic limit (V_{50}) of a cold-rolled AISI 1006 mild steel sheet that has a thickness of 1.50 millimeters (0.0590551 inch):

$$V_{50} = \sqrt{[(D^3 \div M) \times (T \div KD)^{1.250}]}$$

$$V_{50} = \sqrt{[(0.355^3 \div 115) \times (0.0590551 \div (9.35 \times 10^{-9} \times 0.355))^{1.250}]}$$

$$V_{50} = \sqrt{[(0.044738875 \div 115) \times (0.0590551 \div (9.35 \times 10^{-9} \times 0.355))^{1.250}]}$$

$$V_{50} = \sqrt{[3.890336957 \times 10^{-4} \times (17{,}791{,}699.932)^{1.250}]}$$

$$V_{50} = \sqrt{[3.890336957 \times 10^{-4} \times 1{,}155{,}504{,}940.3718]}$$

$$V_{50} = 670.4703 \text{ feet per second}$$
$$(204.3593 \text{ meters per second}).$$

Determine the residual velocity (V_r) of a 9-millimeter (0.355 inch), full metal jacket round nose bullet, weighing 115 grains and having an impact velocity (V_i) of 1,175 feet per second, after it penetrates a cold-rolled

AISI 1006 mild steel sheet that has a thickness of 1.50 millimeters (0.0590551 inch):

$$V_r = \sqrt{[V_i^2 - V_{50}^2]}$$

$$V_r = \sqrt{[(1{,}175)^2 - (670.4703)^2]}$$

$$V_r = \sqrt{[(1{,}380{,}625) - (449{,}530.4232)]}$$

$$V_r = \sqrt{[931{,}094.5768]}$$

$$V_r = 964.9324 \text{ feet per second}$$
$$(294.1114 \text{ meters per second}).$$

After passing through a 1.50-millimeter (0.0590551 inch), cold-rolled AISI 1006 mild steel sheet, to what depth would a 9-millimeter (0.355 inch), 115-grain (7.452 grams), full metal jacket round nose bullet, having an impact (residual) velocity of 964.9324 feet per second (294.1114 meters per second), penetrate in soft tissue that has a density of 1,040 ± 20 kg/m³?

First, determine the value of the uniaxial strain proportionality, ϵ:

$$\epsilon = {}^3\sqrt{D_{mm}} \times \sqrt{(\sigma_t \div \rho_t)}$$

$$\epsilon = {}^3\sqrt{9.017} \times \sqrt{(1{,}000{,}000 \div 1{,}040)}$$

$$c = {}^3\sqrt{9.017} \times \sqrt{(961.538462)}$$

$$\epsilon = 2.081392682 \times 31.008684$$
$$\epsilon = 64.5412.$$

Using the calculated value for ϵ, predict the maximum penetration depth of the 9-millimeter (0.355 inch), full metal jacket round nose bullet, weighing 115 grains (7.452 grams) and having an impact (residual) velocity of 964.9324 feet per second (294.1114 meters per second), in soft tissue that has a density of 1.040 grams per cubic centimeter:

$$S = LN [(V_i \div \epsilon)^2 + 1] \times [M \div (\pi \times (\tfrac{1}{2}D_{cm})^2 \times \rho \times C_D)]$$

$$S = LN [(294.1114 \div 64.5412)^2 + 1] \times [7.452 \div (3.1415927 \times (\tfrac{1}{2} \times 0.9017)^2 \times 1.040 \times 0.573576)]$$

$$S = LN [(4.5570)^2 + 1] \times [7.452 \div (0.3809)]$$

$$S = LN [21.7662] \times [19.5642]$$

$$S = 3.0804 \times 19.5642$$

$$S = 60.2656 \text{ centimeters or } 23.7266 \text{ inches.}$$

As can be seen from the example provided, handgun projectiles are capable of producing deep terminal penetration in soft tissue even after passing through cold-rolled mild steel sheet.

Jacketed hollow point bullets are also capable of such behavior because the walls of their expansion cavities usually, but not always, collapse inward upon themselves during the bullet's passage through cold-rolled mild steel sheet. As a result, expanding projectile designs also possess the potential for deep penetration in soft tissue after passing through hard intermediate barriers.

9

An Expedient Equation

Although the quantitative model is valid and sufficiently accurate, the need for a simpler, more expedient model exists. Such a model may be obtained by fitting it to the same empirical data base that is used to support the quantitative model.

The proposed equation is based upon the structure of the engineering equation found in "PROJECT THOR, Technical Report No. 47: The Resistance of Various Metallic Materials to Perforation by Steel Fragments; Empirical Relationships for Fragment Residual Velocity and Residual Weight". The exponential form of the equation, predicated upon the mathematical argument that terminal ballistic penetration is the product of a projectile's sectional density and its impact velocity, is simple and practical. In adhering to this mathematical argument, the abbreviated equation structure contains the important parameters of projectile areal density, more commonly known as "sectional density", and the projectile's impact velocity. The modified THOR (or *m*THOR) equation accurately predicts the terminal ballistic performance of expanding and non-expanding projectiles in shear-validated 10-percent ordnance gelatin, an extensively researched and highly proven soft tissue simulant.

THOR Equation Modification and Implementation

Since shear-validated 10-percent ordnance gelatin Is the only target material being modeled, the target material variables and exponents were eliminated from the original structure of the THOR equation during the modification process. In order to produce the simplest equation possible while maintaining its predictive accuracy, the exponent for the projectile areal density variable, D_s, was set at 1.00 and the projectile configuration-dependent exponent, α, for the projectile impact velocity variable, V, was fitted to the empirical data for each projectile configuration.

The resulting equation, valid for projectile impact velocities of 300 feet per second to 1,635 feet per second, is predicated upon a constant volumetric density of 1.040 ± 0.020 grams per centimeter^3 for properly shear-validated (8.50 ± 0.40 cm @ 180 ± 4.00 meters per second) 10-percent ordnance gelatin. When evaluated against more than 800 points of independent test data, the modified equation exhibits a very strong correlation of $r = +0.95$, and produces accurate predictions of the terminal penetration depth of expanding and non-expanding projectiles in shear-validated 10-percent ordnance gelatin with a margin of error of one centimeter within a confidence interval of 95 percent.

Since it may be reasonably assumed that a non-expanding design (such as a full metal jacket round nose bullet) will not expand when it is fired into water, the armed professional may simply apply all input variables directly to the equation to obtain a predictive result without undertaking the rigors of testing. Where an actual test of an expanding projectile design (such as a jacketed hollow point bullet) is conducted, the evaluation of the test requires that the projectile's recovered mass (in grains), average recovered radius (in decimal inches), and impact velocity (in feet per second) must be obtained for use in the equation.

As in prior chapters, examples of the *m*THOR equation will be provided to permit the diagnosis and resolution of difficulties that may arise during the implementation of the equation.

The *m*THOR Equation

The *m*THOR equation is presented in this section along with a table of parameter values (α and Φ) and a definition of all variables for the sake of clarity.

Terminal Penetration

$$X_T = D_s \times V^\alpha$$

where $D_s = [(M \div 7{,}000) \div \pi r^2]$

Residual Velocity

$$V_r = [(X_T - T_F) \div (D_s)]^{1/\alpha}$$

Permanent Wound Mass

$$M_{PC} = \pi r^2 X_T \times \Phi \times \rho_{oz}$$

Equation Parameters

Projectile Configuration	α	Φ
Wadcutter	0.6850	1.000000
Jacketed Hollow Point	0.7400	0.819152
Full Metal Jacket Round Nose	0.7200	0.688292
Cruciform Flat Nose	0.7075	0.716610
Truncated Cone	0.7350	0.662324
Semi-Wadcutter	0.7250	0.662324
60° Conical Point	0.7000	0.600000
Round Ball	0.7450	0.497056

Model Variables

D_s = projectile sectional density (pounds per inch^2)
M = (recovered) projectile mass (grains)
M_{PC} = mass within permanent wound cavity (ounces)
r = average (recovered) projectile radius (inches)
T_F = finite target thickness (inches)
V = projectile impact velocity (feet per second)
V_r = residual velocity (feet per second)
X_T = projectile terminal penetration depth (inches)
α = projectile configuration exponent
Φ = projectile configuration factor
$\pi \approx 3.141592653589793$
ρ_{oz} = soft tissue density (0.601158 ounces per inch^3)

The *m*THOR Equation: Operational Constraints

As with the quantitative model, the *m*THOR equation operates under the same three conditions:

- All significant plastic deformation of the projectile occurs within periods of 10^{-4} seconds.

- The projectile behaves as a rigid body after expansion (no further ductile or ablative erosion occurs) and exhibits no significant yaw during any portion of the penetration event.

- The terminal behavior of the projectile is governed by the material strength of the target medium and by the inertial and viscous (or frictional) drag losses that occur during the projectile's penetration through the medium.

Examples

In order to permit the greatest procedural transparency in the following examples, all computations are displayed to an unusually high degree of numerical precision. Conversion of the equation's yields to SI units is accomplished by multiplying its yields, where applicable, by "2.54" to convert inches to centimeters, "0.3048" to convert feet per second to meters per second, and "28.3495" to convert ounces to grams.

<u>Example #1</u>

To what depth would a non-deforming, .45 ACP (diameter = 0.4515 inch), full metal jacket round nose (FMJRN) bullet, weighing 230 grains and having an impact velocity of 835 feet per second, penetrate in soft tissue?

First, determine the sectional density of the 230-grain .45 ACP full metal jacket round nose bullet:

$$D_s = [(M \div 7{,}000) \div \pi r^2]$$

$$D_s = [(230 \div 7{,}000) \div (3.1415927 \times (0.4515 \div 2)^2)]$$

$$D_s = [(230 \div 7{,}000) \div (3.1415927 \times (0.22575)^2)]$$

$$D_s = [(0.03285714) \div (3.1415927 \times (0.05096306))]$$

$$D_s = [0.03285714 \div 0.160105177]$$

$$D_s = 0.205222221$$

Using the calculated value for the sectional density of the .45-caliber 230-grain FMJRN, predict the maximum penetration depth (X_T, in inches) in soft tissue of the non-deforming .45-caliber FMJRN bullet having an impact velocity of 835 feet per second:

$$X_T = D_s \times V^\alpha$$

$$X_T = 0.205222221 \times (835)^{0.7200}$$

$$X_T = 0.205222221 \times 126.944609023$$

$$X_T = 26.051855 \text{ inches (66.1717 centimeters)}$$

At what velocity would the non-deforming, .45-caliber (0.4515 inch), 230-grain, full metal jacket round nose bullet exit an abdomen that has a finite thickness (T_F) of 12.00 inches?

$$V_r = [(X_T - T_F) \div (D_s)]^{1/\alpha}$$

$$V_r = [(26.051855 - 12.00) \div (0.205222221)]^{1/0.7200}$$

$$V_r = [(14.051855) \div (0.205222221)]^{1.38889}$$

$$V_r = [68.4714108]^{1.38889}$$

$$V_r = 354.258663 \text{ feet per second}$$
$$(107.9780 \text{ meters per second})$$

Example #2

A 9mm 115-grain jacketed hollow point bullet fired at a velocity of 1,250 feet per second strikes and passes through an intermediate barrier composed of four layers of denim each having a weight of sixteen ounces per square yard. The denim barrier causes the 9mm JHP bullet to decelerate to a velocity of 1,239 feet per second before striking the water test medium. The 9mm JHP bullet then expands to an average diameter of 0.575 inch upon striking the water test medium and retains 104.5 grains of its original 115-grain weight. How far would the expanded 9mm JHP bullet penetrate in shear-validated 10-percent ordnance gelatin?

First, determine the sectional density of the 9mm JHP bullet using the expanded diameter of the recovered JHP bullet:

$$D_s = [(M \div 7,000) \div \pi r^2]$$

$$D_s = [(104.5 \div 7,000) \div (3.1415927 \times (0.575 \div 2)^2)]$$

$$D_s = [(104.5 \div 7,000) \div (3.1415927 \times (0.2875)^2)]$$

$$D_s = [(0.014928571) \div (3.1415927 \times 0.0826563)]$$

$$D_s = [(0.014928571) \div (0.259672429)]$$

$$D_s = 0.057490012$$

Using the calculated value for the sectional density of the expanded 9mm jacketed hollow point bullet, predict the maximum penetration depth (X_T, in inches) of the 9mm 115-grain jacketed hollow point bullet in shear-validated 10-percent ordnance gelatin using an impact velocity of 1,239 feet per second:

$$X_T = D_s \times V^\alpha$$

$$X_T = 0.057490012 \times (1,239)^{0.7400}$$

$$X_T = 0.057490012 \times 194.4790242$$

$$X_T = 11.180601 \text{ inches (28.3987 centimeters)}$$

Assuming that the expanded 9mm jacketed hollow point bullet was fired into, and remained inside of, an abdomen having a finite thickness (T_F) of 13.00 inches and a soft tissue density of 0.601158 ounces per cubic inch, what would be the total mass (M_{PC}) of permanently crushed soft tissue within the permanent wound cavity produced by the expanded 9mm JHP bullet remaining inside of the abdomen?

Determine the mass (M_{PC}) of permanently damaged soft tissue within the permanent wound cavity produced by the expanded JHP bullet's passage:

$$M_{PC} = \pi r^2 X_T \times \Phi \times \rho_{oz}$$

$$M_{PC} = (0.259672272 \times 11.180601) \times 0.819152 \times 0.601158$$

$$M_{PC} = 2.90329206 \times 0.819152 \times 0.601158$$

$$M_{PC} = 1.429696 \text{ ounces (40.5312 grams)}$$

At what velocity would the expanded 9mm JHP bullet exit an abdomen that has a finite thickness (T_F) of 9.00 inches?

$$V_r = [(X_T - T_F) \div (D_s)]^{1/\alpha}$$

$$V_r = [(11.180601 - 9.00) \div (0.057490012)]^{1/0.7400}$$

$$V_r = [(2.180601) \div (0.057490012)]^{1.35135}$$

$$V_r = [37.93008427]^{1.35135}$$

$$V_r = 136.069180 \text{ feet per second}$$
$$(41.4739 \text{ meters per second})$$

Example #3

A .44 Magnum (diameter = 0.4285 inch) 300-grain hard-cast semi-wadcutter bullet is fired at a velocity of 1,150 feet per second into a block of shear-validated 10-percent ordnance gelatin. Assuming that the bullet does not expand or deform during its penetration through the gelatin block, what would be the maximum penetration depth (X_T) of the .44 Magnum 300-grain semi-wadcutter bullet?

First, determine the sectional density of the .44 Magnum 300-grain hard-cast semi-wadcutter bullet:

$$D_s = [(M \div 7,000) \div \pi r^2]$$

$$D_s = [(300 \div 7,000) \div (3.1415927 \times (0.4285 \div 2)^2)]$$

$$D_s = [(300 \div 7,000) \div (3.1415927 \times (0.21425)^2)]$$

$$D_s = [(0.042857143) \div (3.1415927 \times 0.04590306)]$$

$$D_s = [(0.042857143) \div (0.144208718)]$$

$$D_s = 0.297188294$$

Using the calculated value for the sectional density of the .44 Magnum 300-grain hard-cast semi-wadcutter bullet, predict the maximum penetration depth (X_T, in inches) of the .44 Magnum 300-grain semi-wadcutter bullet in shear-validated 10-percent ordnance gelatin using an impact velocity of 1,150 feet per second:

$$X_T = D_s \times V^\alpha$$

$$X_T = 0.297188294 \times (1,150)^{0.7250}$$

$$X_T = 0.297188294 \times 165.5792588$$

$$X_T = 49.208217 \text{ inches (124.9889 centimeters)}$$

Assume that the .44 Magnum 300-grain hard-cast semi-wadcutter bullet strikes an 11-inch long block of shear-validated 10-percent ordnance gelatin at a velocity of 1,150 feet per second and that the 300-grain semi-wadcutter bullet does not expand or deform as it penetrates the gelatin block. At what velocity would the .44 Magnum 300-grain hard-cast semi-wadcutter bullet emerge from the opposite end of the 11-inch long 10-percent ordnance gelatin block?

$$V_r = [(X_T - T_F) \div (D_s)]^{1/\alpha}$$

$$V_r = [(49.208217 - 11.00) \div (0.297188294)]^{1/0.7250}$$

$$V_r = [(38.208217) \div (0.297188294)]^{1.37931}$$

$$V_r = [128.5656864]^{1.37931}$$

$$V_r = 811.217487 \text{ feet per second}$$
$$(247.2591 \text{ meters per second})$$

The advantages of an efficient mathematical equation that can be solved in less than one minute are difficult to deny. The simplicity, brevity, and accuracy of the *m*THOR equation provides the armed professional with an expedient predictive instrument that immediately yields accurate answers when time and resources are at a premium.

10

Recommendations

Because most armed professionals have never witnessed or been directly involved in the shooting of an armed assailant, the subject of terminal ballistic performance and ammunition selection is approached by many with a sense of uncertainty. This makes the process of selecting ammunition suitable for self-defense more difficult than it ought to be.

Any attempt to describe the relationship of the ballistic wounding mechanism to physical incapacitation through the revision or mitigation of any aspect of the physics and physiology of the ballistic wounding mechanism will result in an inaccurate description of the relationship. The reduction of the underlying physics and physiology of the ballistic wounding mechanism to dimensionless values can only generate equally dimensionless results that are of little practical value to the armed professional. For these reasons, the armed professional interested in the serious evaluation of the terminal ballistic performance of self-defense ammunition should avoid such faulty representations at all costs.

In order for the ballistic wounding mechanism to produce immediate involuntary incapacitation of an assailant whose actions pose a lethal threat, a projectile must strike the assailant where its permanent wound cavity will have an immediate effect upon vital anatomy. The permanent wound cavity must impinge directly upon the central nervous system or violate a large vascular structure in order to produce the involuntary cessation of the assailant's aggressive actions through the irresistible effects of immediate and severe blood pressure loss (hypovolemic shock), the interruption of neurological function, or some combination of both physiological effects.

Because the ballistic wounding mechanism depends directly upon the mass, impact velocity, and expansion of the projectile, the armed professional must decide for himself what specific qualities are the most important to his tactical environment and use those criteria as a basis for selecting the ammunition that best fits his defensive needs. In this chapter, these concerns will be addressed.

Sectional Density

Sectional density (S.D.) is a critical factor in determining the maximum depth to which a projectile in motion will ultimately penetrate in a medium.

The parameter of sectional density is defined as the weight of a projectile divided by the square of the diameter of the projectile in the equation

$$S.D. = (W \div 7,000) \div D^2,$$

where W is the weight of the projectile expressed in grains and D is the diameter of the projectile expressed in decimal inches.

In the simplest example, at identical velocities, a heavy, non-expanding projectile will produce greater penetration than a light, non-expanding projectile of the same diameter and configuration while increasing the velocity of either projectile equally will produce a proportional increase in maximum penetration depth.

With expanding projectile designs such as jacketed hollow point bullets, sectional density decreases upon expansion of the projectile and the decelerative forces acting upon the expansion face of the projectile cause it to behave as a "brake", reducing the terminal penetration of the projectile significantly. This effect is directly proportional to the square of the increase of the projectile's diameter.

Because the expansion of such designs is driven by hydraulic forces that are dependent upon the velocity at which the projectile is driven, greater velocities result in exponentially greater forces accelerating the rate at which projectile expansion proceeds. When an expanding projectile design is driven at a velocity that exceeds its capacity to sustain the deformation produced by the corresponding increase in hydraulic forces, radical expansion may cause the projectile to lose significant mass through excessive fragmentation. A loss of only ten percent of a projectile's initial mass, in conjunction with an inordinate increase in its frontal area (radical expansion) can result in a significant reduction of the projectile's terminal penetration depth, its permanent wound cavity volume, and the damaged soft tissue mass contained therein.

While such terminal ballistic performance serves to ensure that a projectile will be more likely to remain within an assailant's body, it also carries with it the increased risk of penetration insufficient to reach and damage the anatomical structures necessary to produce the immediate incapacitation of an assailant.

For this reason, it is recommended that expanding projectile designs having the greatest possible sectional density be selected over those of lower sectional density.

"Heavy and Slow" vs. "Light and Fast"

Regardless of caliber, when it comes to the selection of self-defense ammunition, tremendous polarization exists between those who favor ammunition that may be characterized as being "heavy and slow" (projectiles of high sectional density driven at subsonic velocities) and those who favor ammunition that may be described as "light and fast" (projectiles of low sectional density driven at supersonic velocities). Despite interminable and sometimes acrimonious debate, neither side may lay claim to being "right" because neither perspective is correct under all conditions, each perspective having its respective advantages and disadvantages.

Those favoring the use of "heavy-for-caliber" projectiles at subsonic velocities argue correctly that, in order to achieve incapacitation, penetration is necessary in order to reach vital organs and structures that lie deep within an assailant's body under conditions where they may be obstructed by a large physique, postural orientation, intermediate physical barriers, or any combination of these factors. Such terminal ballistic performance characteristics may constitute a potential tactical and legal liability where the full frontal presentation of an assailant having a very small physique, absent cover, is encountered and it is impossible to verify a downrange area that is clear of innocents. These liabilities can be mitigated to some extent through a combination of professional training and situational awareness.

Those who prefer the performance of light-weight projectiles driven at supersonic velocities rightfully claim that the increased rate of expansion, resulting from the higher dynamic pressures produced by high-velocity, expanding designs, reduces the potential for injuring or fatally wounding an innocent downrange in the event that a projectile exits an assailant unexpectedly. Mitigation of this tactical and legal liability comes at the risk of inadequate penetration against anatomical and intermediate material barriers and may result in a failure to achieve the immediate incapacitation of an assailant who poses a lethal threat.

Although it is certainly possible to compromise and employ projectiles of moderate sectional density driven at slightly greater than supersonic velocity, any effect upon terminal ballistic performance will probably be negligible unless there is a large variance of sectional densities and velocities within the range of ammunition available for the caliber.

Given that the armed professional is likely to experience unanticipated barriers and conditions during armed encounters, even within his home environment, the selection of projectiles having the greatest possible sectional density is strongly recommended. The armed professional is also strongly encouraged to obtain professional tactical training beyond that mandated by the issuing authority in order to better mitigate the concerns addressed above.

Excessive Penetration and Misses

When an expanding or non-expanding projectile unexpectedly exits an assailant's body, it is said to have "over-penetrated" the target. Because no projectile can exhibit terminal penetration greater than what it is physically capable of producing, the use of this term is somewhat of a misnomer. Excessive penetration, resulting in the exit of a projectile from the body of a violent assailant at a velocity that is great enough to inflict serious physical harm or death upon another, may be mitigated to some extent by the employment of an expanding projectile design.

An additional benefit of employing an expanding projectile design is that, should an expanded projectile unexpectedly exit the body of a violent assailant, its velocity will probably be much lower than that of a non-expanding projectile of equal weight and impact velocity after traversing the same amount of soft tissue. An expanding design will also have a greater skin-penetration threshold velocity after expansion, which means that it will also be less likely to penetrate the body of an innocent bystander downrange should it unexpectedly exit an assailant. An even greater reduction in a projectile's potential for penetration can be attained by employing an expanding projectile of lower sectional density with a higher impact velocity, but exercising this alternative carries with it the risk of inadequate terminal penetration.

The cost of such mitigation comes at the expense of ammunition versatility because terminal penetration may be insufficient to reach the vital structures and organs necessary to produce immediate incapacitation under less-than-optimum conditions. Given the dynamic and unpredictable nature of armed encounters, where brief, obscured target presentation is the rule, rather than the exception, the value of this alternative must be weighed against the attendant risks and conditions specific to the armed professional's tactical environment. The presence of intermediate barriers and innocents in the immediate vicinity or downrange of the armed encounter are elemental considerations that must be considered in the selection of self-defense ammunition.

Of even greater concern is a projectile that completely misses its intended target. When a projectile exits an armed assailant after a well-placed or peripheral strike, it has lost at least some portion of its initial velocity, and may have become aerodynamically destabilized after traversing soft tissue reducing its potential for the infliction of harm or death upon innocents downrange. In stark contrast, a projectile that misses its mark entirely retains most of its initial velocity, remains aerodynamically stable, and constitutes a far greater potential threat for a much greater distance downrange.

All armed professionals must be aware of, prepare, and train for such conditions. These issues are best addressed through a combination of professionally accredited training and the restriction of firearms discharge to situations in which the downrange area is verifiably clear of innocents and bystanders. While it is not without risk to the armed professional, deference to this tactical and ethical principle may be necessary to preserve the life of innocents downrange and must be the foremost consideration in the mind of the armed professional. Adherence to this imperative restriction requires uncommon restraint and discipline and sometimes comes at terrible expense to those who must persevere in insoluble situations even when a "tactically-correct" decision is made.

Terminal Penetration

The determination of terminal penetration appropriate to the armed professional's specific environment requires the careful assessment of potential assailant physiques most likely to be encountered by the armed professional. Other factors that must be considered are the composition and presence of penetrable and impenetrable barriers in the armed professional's environment and the proximity of innocents that may be at risk of being struck by projectiles that either pass through, or completely miss, their intended target.

As the general population's morphology trends toward larger individuals, resulting primarily from an increased rate of obesity, the amount of penetration necessary to reach and effect the vital structures necessary to produce the immediate physical

85

incapacitation of a potential assailant increases. Besides the need to traverse the additional bulk of fat or muscle tissue, other anatomical barriers (such as the upraised arms of an armed assailant) may create conditions that require a projectile to penetrate farther than would normally be required. Once potential assailant stature and physique begins to increase or the presence of intermediate barriers becomes an element of the armed professional's environment, terminal penetration must necessarily increase or the probability of experiencing penetration insufficient to produce immediate incapacitation increases. The solution to this problem is to employ ammunition that provides greater than minimum required penetration.

Generally, ammunition that provides shallow penetration (less than twelve inches) is acceptable only where it will be used against subjects of smaller stature and where perfect, unobstructed, frontal target presentations can be guaranteed or where terminal penetration must be mitigated due to environmental conditions. In such instances, the presence of even the lightest intermediate barriers may pose a serious tactical problem for the armed professional employing such ammunition. Although non-deforming projectile configurations (FMJs, wadcutters) are capable of defeating heavier than anticipated barriers, they are also capable of producing terminal penetration far in excess of the recommended maximum of eighteen inches even after defeating such obstacles. Because of this, the use of non-expanding ammunition designs for the purpose of self-defense should be strictly avoided except where mandated by law. In environments where such conditions exist, an expanding design that produces moderate penetration (fourteen to eighteen inches) after expansion is highly recommended in order to ensure that the ammunition selected can defeat unanticipated obstructions while retaining the ability to produce enough penetration to reach the critical structures and vital organs of an armed assailant.

Modeling Involuntary Incapacitation

Another advantage of mathematical modeling is the ability to model the expenditure of projectile kinetic energy with respect to instantaneous projectile position. This capability can be used to predict a projectile's probability of producing involuntary incapacitation— symbolically defined as $P_{[I/H]}$.

The U.S. Army Ballistic Research Laboratory (BRL) at Aberdeen Proving Grounds has devised a personnel incapacitation model that is strongly correlated to 7,898 WDMET (Wound Data Munitions Effectiveness Team) wound data that relies upon the incremental kinetic energy expenditure over a penetration depth of 1 to 15 centimeters, or ΔE_{15}, of a random projectile strike to the center of mass (COM) of an assailant to predict a projectile's probability of producing involuntary incapacitation. Using the residual velocity equations of the two mathematical terminal ballistic performance models proposed earlier, the respective instantaneous velocities and kinetic energies of projectiles at penetration depths of 1 and 15 centimeters can be used to compute ΔE_{15} for use in the U.S. Army BRL personnel incapacitation model to predict the probability of involuntary incapacitation, or $P_{[I/H]}$, resulting from a random projectile strike to the center of mass (torso/abdomen) of an assailant.

The U.S. Army BRL personnel incapacitation model relies upon empirical coefficients to compute the probability of involuntary incapacitation of assailants in "Assault" and "Defense" modalities ($\leq$ 30 seconds):

$$P_{[I/H]} = [1 + e^{-(-a + b(\log_\Delta E_{15}))}]^{-1}$$

Assault: 100% incapacitation ($\leqq$ 30 seconds)
a = 3.023
b = 1.651
e ≈ 2.718281828459045

Defense: 100% incapacitation ($\leqq$ 30 seconds)
a = 5.825
b = 1.624
e ≈ 2.718281828459045

By way of example, a non-expanding .45 ACP FMJRN bullet weighing 230 grains with an impact velocity of 850 feet per second and a maximum predicted penetration depth of 25.6133 inches (65.0578 centimeters) would have an instantaneous velocity of 831.3285 feet per second and a kinetic energy of 352.8901 foot·pounds at 1 centimeter of penetration depth. At 15 centimeters of penetration depth, the .45 ACP FMJRN bullet would have an instantaneous velocity of 603.5602 feet per second and a kinetic energy of 186.0096 foot·pounds.

Subtracting the instantaneous kinetic energy possessed by the .45 ACP FMJRN projectile at a depth of 15 centimeters from the instantaneous kinetic energy possessed by the projectile at a depth of 1 centimeter yields an incremental kinetic energy expenditure (ΔE_{15}) of 166.8805 foot·pounds. This value of ΔE_{15}, 166.8805 foot·pounds, when applied to the BRL personnel incapacitation model using the "Assault" coefficients for computing the probability of individual incapacitation within a period of 30 seconds, yields the probability of incapacitation produced by a single .45 ACP FMJRN projectile striking an individual assailant in the center of mass (torso/abdomen) as:

$$P_{[I/H]} = [1 + e^{-(-a + b(\log_{\Delta}E_{15}))}]^{-1}$$

$$P_{[I/H]} = [1 + e^{-(-3.023 + 1.651(\log(166.8805)))}]^{-1}$$

$$P_{[I/H]} = [1 + e^{-(-3.023 + 1.651(2.222405592)}]^{-1}$$

$$P_{[I/H]} = [1 + e^{-(-3.023 + 3.669191633)}]^{-1}$$

$$P_{[I/H]} = [1 + 2.718281828459045^{-0.646191632}]^{-1}$$

$$P_{[I/H]} = [1.524037709]^{-1}$$

$$P_{[I/H]} = 0.656151743 \text{ or } 65.6151743\%$$

Expanding ammunition designs, like JHPs, increase the probability of incapacitation ($P_{[I/H]}$) by increasing the amount of stress produced in adjacent tissues. The larger frontal area of an expanded JHP bullet produces greater stresses that result in greater strain energy storage within the surrounding tissues increasing tissue damage and the probability of incapacitation. A .45 ACP JHP bullet having the same mass and impact velocity as the .45 ACP FMJRN bullet in the prior example that expands to 1.5 times its original diameter (or 0.675 inch) will produce greater tissue-damaging stresses than a non-expanding FMJRN design.

For example, a .45 ACP JHP bullet weighing 230 grains with an impact velocity of 850 feet per second that expands to an (average) expanded diameter of 0.675 inch would have a maximum predicted penetration depth of 13.5180 inches (34.3357 centimeters). At 1 centimeter of penetration depth, the .45 ACP JHP would have an instantaneous velocity of 817.4166 feet per second and an instantaneous kinetic energy of 341.1780 foot·pounds. At 15 centimeters of penetration depth, the .45 ACP JHP would have an instantaneous velocity of 451.0504 feet per second and an instantaneous kinetic energy of 103.8830 foot·pounds. Subtracting the instantaneous kinetic energy possessed by the .45 ACP JHP projectile at a depth of 15 centimeters from the instantaneous kinetic energy possessed by the .45 ACP JHP projectile at a depth of 1 centimeter yields an incremental kinetic energy expenditure (ΔE_{15}) of 237.2950 foot·pounds. This value of ΔE_{15}, 237.2950 foot·pounds, when applied to the BRL personnel incapacitation model using the "Assault" coefficients for computing the probability of individual incapacitation within a period of 30 seconds, yields the probability of incapacitation produced by a single expanded .45 ACP JHP projectile striking an individual assailant in the center of mass (torso/abdomen) as:

$$P_{[I/H]} = [1 + e^{-(-a + b(\log\Delta E_{15}))}]^{-1}$$

$$P_{[I/H]} = [1 + e^{-(-3.023 + 1.651(\log(237.2950)))}]^{-1}$$

$$P_{[I/H]} = [1 + e^{-(-3.023 + 1.651(2.375288587)}]^{-1}$$

$$P_{[I/H]} = [1 + e^{-(-3.023 + 3.921601457)}]^{-1}$$

$$P_{[I/H]} = [1 + 2.718281828459045^{-0.898601458}]^{-1}$$

$$P_{[I/H]} = [1.407138662]^{-1}$$

$$P_{[I/H]} = 0.710662017 \text{ or } 71.10662017\%$$

The advantage of employing JHP ammunition (that expands reliably) for defensive use is undeniable. The larger frontal area of the expanded .45 ACP 230-grain JHP bullet produces a greater rate of incremental kinetic energy expenditure (ΔE_{15}) than the .45 ACP 230-grain FMJRN. This increased rate of incremental kinetic energy expenditure produces greater strain energy storage stresses in tissues adjacent to the projectile's path that result in a higher probability of tissue damage and a subsequent $P_{[I/H]}$ that is 8.308% greater than the $P_{[I/H]}$ produced by the non-expanding .45 ACP 230-grain FMJRN in the prior example.

Summary Recommendation

While it is impossible to make a recommendation that is appropriate for every possible contingency, JHP ammunition suitable for general-purpose usage should:

- possess the highest practical sectional density obtainable

- have a muzzle velocity between 800 and 1,100 feet per second

- produce 16.00 ± 2.00 inches of terminal penetration regardless of barrier(s) encountered

Ultimately, the armed professional is responsible for the selection of self-defense ammunition that is most appropriate to their specific tactical environment. The mathematical terminal ballistic performance modeling described herein is proposed in the hope that it will allow both armed professionals and under-funded law enforcement agencies to employ a scientifically valid process to test, evaluate, and select appropriate self-defense ammunition.

References

Newton, Sir Isaac. *Philosophiæ Naturalis Principia Mathematica*, 1687.

Fackler, Dr. Martin L. and Kneubuehl, Beat P. "Applied Wound Ballistics: What's New and What's True" San Francisco: Letterman Army Institute of Research, 1990.

Hatcher, General Julian S. *Textbook of Pistols and Revolvers: Their Ammunition, Ballistics, and Use*, 1935.

Hudgins, Henry. "Estimating Ballistic Limits of Skin and Clothing for Projectiles" GARM Conference, 40th Annual Armament Systems, 2005.

Johns Hopkins University. "The Resistance of Various Metallic Materials to Perforation by Steel Fragments; Empirical Relationships for Fragment Residual Velocity and Residual Weight" Technical Report No. 47, Ballistic Analysis Laboratory, Institute for Cooperative Research, Project THOR, 1961.

Thoresby, Major F. P. "Armalite Rifle (AR15) Wound Ballistics Trials" Porton Technical Paper No. 904, Chemical Defence Experimental Establishment, 1964.

Neades, David N. and Prather, Russell N. "The Modeling and Application of Small Arms Wound Ballistics" U.S. Army Ballistic Research Laboratory, Aberdeen Proving Grounds, MD, 21005-5066, 1991.

Printed in the United States
by Baker & Taylor Publisher Services